BE THE HERO
OF YOUR LIFE

DITCH THE EXCUSES, TAKE YOUR HERO'S JOURNEY,

AND FIND YOUR LIFE'S PURPOSE

Mobes Publishing
www.mobespublishing.com

ISBN: 978-1-7334096-0-5 (print)
ISBN: 978-1-7334096-1-2(ebook)

Ordering Information:
Special discounts are available on quantity purchases by corporations, associations, and others. For details, contact www.mobespublishing.com

CONTENTS

BE THE HERO
OF YOUR LIFE

DITCH THE EXCUSES, TAKE YOUR HERO'S JOURNEY,

AND FIND YOUR LIFE'S PURPOSE

J. SCOTT MACMILLAN

INTRODUCTION
HOW THE HERO'S JOURNEY CAN HELP
YOU ACHIEVE YOUR PURPOSE

In the summer of 2001, I was in the shower when I suddenly heard a voice in my head that said, "This is not the way to live life—you must be doing something wrong."

Life had just spiraled out of control. Here I was, living in a beautiful house, in a great city, with a wife, two healthy children, and a good corporate job, yet I was miserable. My health was failing, my marriage was falling apart, and my job had become stagnant and unfulfilling. I was simply going through the motions of life.

That morning, I was hoping the hot water would help relax my extremely painful back and neck muscles. About a year earlier, I had noticed that my right shoulder ached after I played catch with my son, so I made what would become the first of many physical therapy and doctors' appointments. The pain just kept getting worse and was spreading through my back even though I kept trying new doctors and physical therapists. I was exhausted and in constant, chronic pain.

I had even tried a whole host of alternative therapies, including cortisone shots, physical therapy, acupuncture, red light laser therapy, as well as massage and chiropractic therapy techniques.

That morning in 2001 began one of the most significant days of my life, though it would be more than 15 years until I recognized it. It was the day I woke up, focused internally, and stopped blaming the outside world for my problems. I had no clue what to do, but I knew I needed to change my thinking before I could heal and live a healthy and fulfilling life again.

Do you have big hopes, dreams, and aspirations that you haven't been able to achieve? Have fear, doubt, and worry stopped you from doing what you know you are meant to do? Have you found that with each passing year, your regrets seem to grow while your list of dreams and accomplishments never materializes?

Maybe now is the time to make your dreams of being prosperous and fulfilled a reality. Maybe it's time to have more clarity and confidence in your work and your life, uncover your purpose, and live the life of your dreams. Anyone who knows there is more to life than what they are currently experiencing will want to read this book. Many people know they are stuck but don't know how to get unstuck—how to find their purpose and move forward.

I stumbled upon the "hero's journey" concept while I was studying documentary filmmaking. It was originally attributed to the mythologist Joseph Campbell but has been refined by many authors and scholars to depict a common theme used in all stories and movies. As you will see, by using Campbell's initial concept of a hero's journey as a map of your own life, you will understand who you truly are and that you've always been the hero in your own life story. Learning about what makes us tick enhances our self-motivation and self-management, resulting in self-respect.

So how did I do it? Read on. This book is the final stage of my first hero's journey because as you will see, the journey ends with the sharing of your story with others, thereby helping them identify their own story, and thus begin the process of finding their purpose and living their true authentic lives. And then we start our next journey with new powers and insights.

I am just an average guy with an uneventful life. I have little to complain about and my suffering pales in comparison to that of many others. I know I'm not alone. I feel there may be a lot of us who have had nice lives, yet still get stuck and suffer. We all suffer, but some have the capacity to let things go and forge on while others can't.

It's my hope that after reading my story, you will realize you are a hero—the hero of your own story. I hope that you will answer the call to take your own hero's journey, thereby finding health, happiness, and a fulfilling, purpose-driven life.

In this book, we'll dissect the stages of the hero's journey. I have included examples from some of our favorite movies to show how Hollywood uses the hero's journey as a story structure. For each stage I will also detail my personal hero's journey which can be used as an example when it's your turn to put your life into the hero's journey.

You will be able to place yourself into your own hero's journey. You will learn to identify how your life has been influenced by each stage of the journey and where in your life you have identified with the hero. Finally, you will understand that you have done the best you could at the time which allows you to be the hero of your own life. You see, when we realize that our life has made us who we are today, we begin to feel empowered to take risks, start trusting our internal guidance, and truly live our best authentic life.

In addition to understanding and healing, you will also learn about powerful guided meditations, visualizations, and thought-provoking exercises you can use to help you fully integrate the lessons learned on your journey. These exercises and tools are designed to help you understand past traumas and fully heal as you move from one stage to the next.

We will explore ancient principles of human thought and consciousness to help us recognize that how we think dictates how we live. Once you know the path of your hero's journey, you will need to apply the latest research on how to live a genuinely extraordinary life. We will then dive into the amazing scientific work of Dr. Joe Dispenza and his Quantum Thinking model where we will learn to train our brains to think differently.

If you've been stuck or feel there is more to life, it's most likely because you've been focusing on symptoms instead of getting to the root cause of your suffering. Learning about your own hero's journey will help you discover why you're stuck, and help you heal and move forward so you can begin living your true, authentic, and purposeful life.

The only difference between people who truly thrive in all areas of life and those who are stuck and stagnate is that the former have heard the call to adventure and stepped out of their comfortable, ordinary world to begin walking forward into their hero's journey.

The hero's journey asks you to answer the call and move from your ordinary world into an unknown world. It is not only the thing you fear the most but it's real work. And it's hard—but you can do it. You know you must do it. Joseph Campbell once said, "The cave you fear to enter holds the treasure you seek."

You have a deep understanding that there is something of more significance for you and you're finally ready to figure it out. To find and live your true authentic life though, you've got to wander through the desert of your traumas. You've got to get to the root cause of what's kept you stuck and be more honest then you probably have ever been with yourself. You've got to face your biggest fear, stare it right in the face, and walk through it. This is serious work. But it will pay off in the highest rewards this life has to offer. It will not be easy. You will want to quit, and you will make a lot of mistakes. It's going to be messy and scary. But that's okay. Don't give up—stay with this process and see it through. Your life depends on it.

For downloadable PDF exercises and videos on being the hero of your life visit http://www.betheheroofyourlife.com/downloads/.

SECTION ONE
THE HERO'S JOURNEY

CHAPTER 1
WHAT IS THE HERO'S JOURNEY?

Joseph Campbell, an American scholar and mythologist, identified a basic narrative that appears in drama, storytelling, myth, and religious ritual. He studied all the indigenous and cultural myths and stories of the world, and found there is one main storyline that exists within all of them: it describes the typical adventure of the archetype known as "the hero."

In his study of the archetypal myth of the hero, Campbell suggests the existence of a monomyth, a universal pattern that is the essence of, and is common to, heroic tales in every culture. The main character, the hero, goes out and achieves great deeds on behalf of himself, a group, or civilization. Many writers, as well as popular movies like *The Wizard of Oz, Star Wars, Superman, The Godfather, Titanic, and Avatar* — have used the framework of the hero's journey. The character archetypes we see in our modern action hero movies are essentially contemporary versions of ancient myths.

Campbell's classic version has three main phases: Departure, Initiation, and Return.

Departure: The hero is in one form of reality, then is suddenly separated from it. The hero receives a call to action, gains a mentor, and learns of their destiny.

Initiation: The hero comes into their own, faces and overcomes problems, then finally meets their match and receives a renewed sense of purpose.

Return: The hero accepts their responsibility, gains some magical help, slays some dragons, and returns home with treasure and stories.

I've adapted Campbell's classic version to suit a journey of personal development and retitled the three main phases the Preparation, the Journey, and the Return.

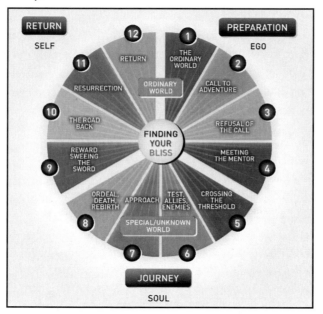

THE HERO'S JOURNEY MAP

THIS GRAPHIC SHOWS THE 12 STAGES OF THE HERO'S JOURNEY. THE JOURNEY IS DEPICTED AS A CIRCLE BECAUSE THE HERO MUST ALWAYS RETURN TO BRING BOTH THE TREASURE OF THE VICTORY AND THE STORIES HOME SO OTHERS MAY FIND AND PARTAKE IN THEIR OWN HERO'S JOURNEY. IT ALSO LISTS THE THREE MAIN PHASES (PREPARATION, JOURNEY, AND RETURN) AND HOW THEY LINE UP WITH CARL JUNG'S PERSONAL DEVELOPMENTAL MODEL OF THE EGO, SOUL, AND SELF. IN ADDITION, IT DELINEATES WHICH STAGES ARE IN THE ORDINARY OR SPECIAL WORLD.

Great hero movies call on the hero within all of us when we watch them. For Dorothy in *The Wizard of Oz*, it wasn't just about defeating the wicked witch, it was about claiming her own inner resources. At the end of the movie, she realized she had the ability to get back home all along by clicking her heels; she just needed to go through the trials and tribulations to come to that realization.

The key to using the hero's journey as a light in our lives is to embrace metaphor. We've all heard the story about the knights of the round table and their epic search for the Holy Grail. The story is not about the grail itself; it's about the metaphor for that intangible feeling they are searching for. Metaphors instruct us on how to lead an extraordinary and fulfilling life by embedding wisdom and information within the content of the story.

Once we are taught about a mythical character, just thinking of that character invokes their entire story and its meaning. Carl Jung, one of the fathers of modern psychology, called these "archetypes." These are encapsulated stories that plant a seed in our collective unconscious. When that archetypal idea is planted, it starts to sprout. It brings forth the relationships and patterns that help the story we are journeying through unfold. According to Jung, the collective unconscious is the repository of all symbols and experiences of religion, spirituality, and mythology. These archetypal images are ingrained in our understanding before birth, and they become the conceptual patterns behind all our thinking and beliefs.

It's much easier to tell a story to help explain life than just simply giving an explanation. Stories are richer and move deeper into our psyche. So it's possible to follow these hero stories, see ourselves in them, and therefore manifest the reality of the hero moving through a journey to reap a reward. In mythology, the hero's journey chronicles the notion that all mystical traditions call us to a deeper understanding of the act of living. Myths and stories guide us through trials and traumas from birth to death.

We are all capable of finding meaning and purpose in our lives, and in the hero's journey, we find a model for learning how to live in stories about heroism. The hero's journey is about saying yes to yourself and becoming more fully alive and effective in the world. The hero's journey is mainly about taking a journey to find the treasure of your authentic self, and then about returning home to tell your story to help transform the kingdom, village, or community you inhabit and in the process, your own life. The journey is fraught with dangers like metaphorical dragons and ogres that we must slay so we can reap the rewards of the knowledge we can gain by finding our unique gifts. We never stop journeying. Each time we begin our journey, we do so at a new level and return with new treasure and newfound transformative abilities. Thus, the hero's journey comes full circle.

Heroes come in all shapes and sizes. Some are adventurous, while others shun the hero label. Some start out weak, some start strong. Some are family oriented while others are loners. Heroes are far from perfect; they have flaws like we all do. The essence of what makes a hero though, is the willingness to serve others and give of themselves for the greater good.

Follow Your Bliss

Campbell talks about "following your bliss" as the essence of the hero's journey. To follow your bliss means to follow your heart and follow your truth. According to Campbell, bliss is not ecstasy or happiness. There is a serenity in bliss. It's the thing that you can't not do. It's your authentic self calling you to find your soul's life purpose and live in it. It's about doing what makes you feel most alive. Embarking on your hero's journey is to have the courage to look within and ask yourself: What am I here to do? What am I most passionate about in my life? What are my greatest gifts, and how do I give them to the world?

"Life has no meaning," Campbell said. "Each of us has meaning and we bring it to life. It is a waste to be asking the question when you are the answer."

Stories about heroes link our own path with those who have come before us in such a way that we learn something about what it means to be human. As we explore the stages of the hero's journey, we'll look at some popular movies and see how they match up with Campbell's stages. We will see how they can be compared to examples of ordinary people becoming heroes. I'll also share the stages of my own hero's journey so you can follow me on the healing path.

CHAPTER 2
JUNG'S DEVELOPMENTAL MODEL —
THE EGO, THE SOUL, AND THE SELF

The three phases of the hero's journey that I call Preparation, Journey, and Return line up perfectly with the three elements of personality development described in Carl Jung's developmental model—the ego, the soul, and the self. Jung, a pioneering psychiatrist who founded analytical psychology in the mid-1900s, called this process of developing the personality the "individuation process."

The Ego

According to Jung, the ego shows us how to be safe and successful in the world, while the soul helps us become authentic as we explore the mysteries of life. The journey of the self illustrates how we can shine in our authenticity, power, and freedom.

In the first stage of the hero's journey, Preparation, the ego comes directly into play. It is the time when the hero prepares to leave a comfortable and stable environment and develops inner resources necessary to go out into the world on their own. On the journey, the hero discovers their true gifts. The Return is when the hero comes back to the community to share these gifts and live with others in a state of interdependence.

Carol Pearson, author of Awakening the Heroes Within, explains that in Jung's developmental model, the ego is the "platform" for our life. It creates the boundaries between us and everything else and mediates our relationship with the world. It shows us how to fit into the world and to act to change that world to better meet our needs. The soul connects us with the spiritual. It is also the pure potential of human beings, like seeds germinating and ready to sprout if external conditions are prosperous. The self is our sense of our identity. When the self is born, we finally know who we are; we experience wholeness and integrity. We then try to find ways to express ourselves in the world, and in doing so, make contributions that only we alone can make to bring joy and authenticity to our lives.

The Soul

The soul connects us with that part of us that needs to explore and to find ourselves. To push the limits and find our potential. The soul is also our spiritual connection and directly connected to intimacy with another person. During times of crisis, the soul yearns for meaning and often seeks out meaningful events and situations. As seen in mythological stories, many cultures have developed rituals to mark the transition in and out of these deeper spiritual times.

The Self

The self is the expression of wholeness and the last part of Jung's developmental model. The journey has been completed and your being has been transformed. The self is the entry point into a new way of living. We become the kings and queens of our metaphorical kingdoms. But we must integrate the wisdom of the journey into our consciousness for us to fully claim our thrones.

The hero's journey is about personal growth. By connecting it to Jung's developmental stages we can identify how mature we become as we move through the stages or where we are stuck and need more time in a particular stage.

Comparing Developmental Tasks and Outcomes

As we explore the hero's journey and map it to Jung's developmental model, we can see, as the table shows, the basic healthy developmental tasks and outcomes that are achieved from each developmental stage (ego, soul, self). For example, when we move from the ego stage to the soul stage, a healthy ego should have learned how to care for the self and others. Therefore, as we study and explore our own developmental stages, we may find we need healing work in our ego stage before we can truly move into our soul and self-stages.

Once we have reviewed and identified ourselves in this formula, we can begin to see where understanding and healing needs to occur so that we can claim the treasure of living as our true authentic selves and find our purpose in life.

Phase of the Journey	Preparation	Journey	Return
Human Development	Ego	Soul	Self
Outcome	Caring for yourself and getting along with others	Finding your gifts, values, and purpose	Sharing your gifts with others and living with integrity

Developmental Tasks	Develop Trust	Create Identity	Share Gifts
	Develop trust in self and others	Find what you love	Actively share your gifts with others
	Become Autonomous	**Establish Intimacy**	**Establish Authenticity**
	Stand up for, protect, and defend the self	Find whom you love and being willing to commit and let go	Be true to yourself and claiming your own wisdom
	Take Initiative		
	Learn to take responsibility for yourself		
	Be Industrious		
	Learn basic social skills and work habits		
The Twelve Stages of the Hero's Journey	The Ordinary World	Crossing the Threshold	The Reward
	The Call to Adventure	Test, Allies, and Enemies	The Road Back
	Refusal of the Call	The Approach	The Resurrection
	Meeting the Mentor	The Ordeal	Return with the Treasure

Adapted from Patricia R. Adson and Carol S. Pearson

Myth versus Personal Development

Before we look at the 12 stages of the hero's journey, I want to clarify that we will be comparing the myth, story, and structure of outer world conquests we see in the movies to the inner journey of personal development. For the purposes of self-discovery, we no longer want to view the hero's journey map as a representation of a physical place. We want to go inside ourselves and uncover our true, authentic, and purpose-driven life by understanding our feelings and emotions and how they have contributed to our life so far.

Referring to the twelve stages of the hero's journey and the division of the ordinary world from the special world, it's helpful to equate our conscious mind with the ordinary world (the known), and our subconscious mind with the special world (the unknown). These subtle changes enable us to adapt Campbell's mythically based hero's journey from stories and movies to personal growth and development.

CHAPTER 3

PHASE 1 — THE PREPARATION

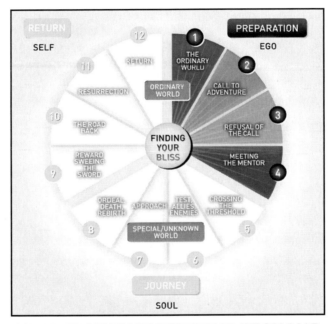

THE HERO'S JOURNEY PREPARATION MAP

In the Preparation phase of the hero's journey, the first four stages are The Ordinary World, The Call to Adventure, Refusal of the Call, and Meeting the Mentor. These four stages represent preparation for the journey ahead. When we compare the stages of the hero's journey to Jung's first developmental stage, we see that the ego teaches us how to be safe and successful in the world, which prepares us for our journey. The hero is often said to be the archetype of the ego, but this is only partially true. The hero's journey encompasses all the developmental stages. Establishing a healthy ego, however, is the prerequisite for taking the journey safely.

We come into this world, small, fragile, and helpless with our ego unformed. We are left in the care of parents or other adults who try hard but don't always know what we need. As we gain control over our lives, we begin to learn what we can do and how we can affect what happens to us. With this awareness, the ego is born.

Jung points out that no matter how old or wise or mature we are, we were all vulnerable children and we still bear the scars of our formative years. The ego's first task is to protect the inner child. At some point during childhood, the ego begins to take on the protective function from the parent and gradually with maturation assumes that task completely. The ego's next task, and its basic function, is to mediate our relationship with the outside world.

The stories we identify with most are those about ego development. The classic hero on a white horse, the knight slaying the dragon, and Luke Skywalker defeating Darth Vader are all versions of the classic story of the ego. The hero and the kingdom are in danger from some hostile force. The key to the hero's success is having the courage and ability to defend the gates. The hero is often a conqueror, the person who goes after what they want. Carol Pearson eloquently puts it this way, "The capacity to get what we want and protect our boundaries does not, in itself, make us heroes… What makes a hero is a nobility of spirit manifested as concern and compassion for others."

It's not enough to go after what you want. To be a hero, your conquests must be in service to others as well. Pearson goes on to explain, "Preparation for the journey requires each of us to be socialized adequately, be effective in society and then separate from the world enough to assert independent values, opinions, and desires. Finally, it demands that we use this capacity for autonomy and independence, not simply for selfish ends—although we do want to seek our own good—we seek for the good of the whole as well."

Stage One: The Ordinary World—Where You Are Now

According to Campbell's theory, in stories and myth, the ordinary world is where the hero is introduced in a basic and sympathetic way so the audience can identify with the situation or dilemma. The ordinary world is the baseline—the status quo. It may not be pretty or exactly the way we want it, but for better or worse, it is the starting point. There is polarity, though, in the hero's life that pulls him or her in different directions and causes stress. A hidden part of us hints at change, seeks a renewed spirit, and foresees a better future.

In the 1977 movie, *Star Wars: Episode IV - A New Hope,* we are introduced to Luke Skywalker, played by Mark Hamill, who languishes in his ordinary world, knowing there is more for him. Joseph Campbell praised the movie's creator and director, George Lucas, as a master storyteller using all the classic stages of the hero's journey in his epic *Star Wars* movies. We meet our first reluctant hero on a desert planet where he lives with his aunt and uncle, who took him in after his father disappeared. As he does his daily chores of repairing and maintaining moisture farming droids, he longs for more. He stands on a bluff as the twin suns of Tatooine are setting and gazes out to the horizon, wishing he could become a pilot and escape the dusty planet.

We all start our Journey in our ordinary world. For Luke Skywalker it was a dusty planet. For you it may be a small town that you can't wait to leave after you finish school. Or your ordinary world may be a bad marriage filled with fighting and abuse, and your journey consists of finding a way out of that situation.

Stage one is the ordinary world where your journey starts. It's where you are living your life. It may be good or bad, but things are about to change, as the call to adventure is just around the corner.

Unlike Luke, my ordinary world wasn't on a desert planet but suburban America. I lived with my wife and kids and had a good but stressful corporate job. We had just moved from northern Virginia where I was an engineer and corporate trainer. Life certainly appeared wonderful, and it was for the first three years in our new house. My wife was able to stay home to raise the kids and I was climbing the corporate ladder. We had been married for 11 years at the time I had my morning shower voice experience, but what happened before that was what I call the "blind time." I was blindly following the American dream with my head down, working hard, raising kids, and not paying attention to my stress levels, my body, or anything other than striving to make the American dream come true—whatever that was. Don't get me wrong, it's not that I wasn't enjoying life. I was coaching my kids in sports and enjoying friends and family on the weekends and holidays, but all along, the stress monster was eating away at my mind and body, and I had no idea it was happening.

Campbell explains that in the earliest stage of the hero's journey, we live in the present day, but we are uneasy and uncomfortable and unaware that there is something else out there waiting for us, or that there is another way to behave or react to everyday events.

The hero's home is the "safe haven" to which the special world and the journey's outcome can be compared. The hero begins the journey in the ordinary world, travels to the special world, and then returns to the ordinary world. As we go through Campbell's stages, remember that it's helpful to equate the ordinary world with our conscious mind and the special world with the subconscious mind. We start out living in our normal conscious mind world until something happens to us and we have to look inside at our subconscious mind to find the answers to why we are behaving a certain way.

Campbell also believes that most of us live with the illusion that the life we are living is all there is. For many of us, our lives are filled with media bombardment and consumerism. We are lured into a trance of comfort, not wanting to stick our heads out too far. So as heroes, we are confronted with the fact that the reality we thought was real—consumerism and comfort—isn't real. Therefore, we must not be afraid to go within to find meaning and significance. In our contemporary "more is better" culture, spirituality and personal development are less appreciated, less valued, and less understood than worshiping the outer displays of success.

Stage Two: The Call to Adventure—Great Change in Your Life Is Coming

For the hero, separation from the illusion begins with Stage Two: The Call to Adventure. The phone is ringing. The Universe/God/Creator is literally calling you to step out and live your journey. Something breaks into your reality and makes it impossible for you to continue down your current path. You can ignore the call and not answer, but it will keep calling back until you finally do.

For a lot of us, the wakeup call comes in the form of a sledgehammer. Often, it comes in the depths of our despair, losing a job for example, having a health crisis (like me), getting divorced, or dealing with foreclosure on your house. These aren't the things you want to happen in your life, but they are exactly what you need to awaken and catapult you into the next phase of your journey. The Universe/God/Creator just upended you, knocked you on your ass, and woke you up.

This happened to my client, M.H. After 27 years of marriage, he and his wife divorced, and then he was laid off from work. Needless to say, he was devastated and looking for answers. After working through his hero's journey, he realized that he needed to accept what had happened to him and continue to move forward on his journey to learn the lessons presented before him.

But here is the miracle in this. Your awakening is the opportunity you've been waiting for; you just didn't know it. Did you know that the Chinese symbol for the word "crisis" is composed of two symbols, one meaning danger and the other meaning opportunity? So crisis is both danger and opportunity together.

CHINESE SYMBOL FOR CRISIS

In the 2001 movie, *Harry Potter and the Sorcerer's Stone*, we see Harry Potter, played by Daniel Radcliffe, in his gloomy ordinary world. He is a young boy forced to sleep in a closet by his aunt and uncle, and is constantly tortured by his bratty cousin.

Harry's call to adventure came as a flood of letters of acceptance from Hogwarts School of Witchcraft and Wizardry where Harry's amazing adventures would begin.

The call to adventure comes to all of us at one point in our lives whether we like it or not. We are wired to seek new situations or interests. We naturally seek solutions to problems, so when we hear the call to adventure we instinctively know we must make a change.

My first inkling that something needed to change in my life started on a normal day. I wasn't feeling well that day. I hadn't been feeling well for many weeks, but that day I was feeling especially bad and very lethargic. I came home after work and tried to forget about everything and just get to the next day. I went to bed early but couldn't get to sleep, and at around 2:00 a.m., I woke my wife and told her I needed to go the emergency room because I was having a kidney stone attack. When I was in college, I had my first kidney stone, but it was a gradual and slow, dull pain that would come and go. This pain started slowly but came on strong, and I was sure this was an acute kidney stone attack. So we loaded our kids—who were very young at the time—into the car and headed to the emergency room. It felt like hours before the doctors could see me, run some tests, and finally give me pain medication. By the time they wheeled me into the x-ray room, I was in excruciating pain and don't remember much of anything else until the next morning when I woke up in the hospital with a morphine drip, so thankful the pain was gone. I had passed the stone during the night and thought my problems and pain would soon be over. Oh, was I wrong. They released me later that day and as the pain medication wore off, my stomach still hurt. Not the same kind of dull, achy pain as the kidney stone, but more of a nauseous and stabbing pain that didn't go away for eight months. Those eight months consisted of seeing doctor after doctor and having test after test which showed no traditional signs for the way I was feeling. At that time, when they couldn't diagnose stomach problems, they just assumed it was irritable bowel syndrome. They now have some treatments for that, but at the time, they didn't have any. After trying every diet under the sun to alleviate my pain, as well as losing 25 pounds, the symptoms slowly got better on their own. But here's the kicker: I still didn't know what was going on with me and didn't understand the internal wisdom of the call to adventure that was trying to alert me to change my thinking and my life.

When my stomach pain couldn't get my attention, the divine wisdom in my body found other areas of weakness and trapped emotional trauma to exploit. Later on, we'll discuss how we all have trapped emotional trauma stuck in our bodies that originated in our childhoods that affects our adult lives in many ways. As I mentioned before, I was playing catch with my son one day when I noticed that my arm was particularly sore that night. That soreness grew into a lot of pain that sent me back to the doctor for another examination. Once again, I was back on the treadmill of doctors, MRIs, physical therapists, injections in my neck, and finally, meetings with surgeons who all said I didn't need surgery to fix my back problems. I was getting close to hearing the call because at that point, I decided to stop seeing all doctors and just chill out. I began taking Tai Chi and yoga classes and reading about stress reduction. I started to realize that I needed to reduce my stress and start living my life differently. But it wasn't until that morning in the shower that I actually heard my first call to adventure.

In the classic movie, The Wizard of Oz, which debuted in 1939, Dorothy, played by Judy Garland, is called to adventure when her house falls on the wicked witch and she enters the land of Oz. She has no choice but to follow the yellow brick road (her hero's journey) to find the wizard and get back home. For most of us, our call to adventure is a feeling or a knowing that there is more; while for others, like Dorothy and Harry Potter, the call is a big event that forces you to take your journey.

Stage Three: Refusal of the Call—Fear of the Unknown or Known

Before we cross the threshold to begin our journeys, most of us move into Stage Three, which is the Refusal of the Call. It is very common for the hero to feel the fear of the unknown and try to turn away from the adventure. Who hasn't experienced this? We have a feeling that we should make a change or do something that is out of our comfort zone, but we back away and push that thought out of our head because we are afraid. There are many reasons we refuse the call. We may not know ourselves well enough to recognize it, and even if we do, we may not be ready for it. We may not want it badly enough, or maybe we're not sure the call is for us. One thing is certain though, if we refuse the call, the Universe/God/Creator doesn't give up. We will constantly experience suffering and repeat these patterns until we finally answer the call and cross the threshold into the special world.

One of the funniest movie examples of refusing the call comes from the 1993 movie, Groundhog Day, where actor Bill Murray portrays Phil Conners, a local news reporter who is repeatedly forced to relive a single day until he embraces the call and becomes a better person.

Who hasn't felt like Phil when he wakes up to the same alarm clock radio program and experiences the same day repeatedly? The Universe/God/Creator will continue to remind us that we need to change.

My client, R.C., refused the call over and over in her early adult life. She married a man who constantly verbally abused and gaslighted her, but she continued to stay with him for many months. After she decided to leave him, her church also began verbally abusing her, telling her to go back to her husband and be a good girl.

Like R.C., I also repeatedly refused the call. After I heard the call in the shower that morning, it would be another nine years before I would fully answer, enter my new world by getting divorced, leaving a job of 16 years, and starting my own business. That's a lot of metaphorical death. But those old patterns needed to go so I could heal and rise like a phoenix and claim my true, authentic life.

Stage Four: Meeting with the Mentor—Who Will Help You on the Journey

The last stage in the Preparation phase is Stage Four: Meeting with the Mentor. Before the hero has enough courage and skill to travel on his or her journey, they first come across a seasoned traveler who gives them training, equipment, or advice that will help on the journey. Or one might reach within a source of courage and wisdom. We've all had mentors in one form or another. They are the people we meet who inspire us and give us wisdom that helps us take that step forward. Good mentors don't have to be wise old gray-haired guys; they just need to be a little further down the road to help guide you to the answers within. Mentors almost always appear just as you're about to leave the ordinary world and enter the unknown special world. Mentors also know what the hero desires and needs. While on their own journeys, they have reflected on their successes and failures, which allows them to respect the stage the apprentice is in and why they need to be there.

If the hero's commitment and competence are proven, the mentor may reward the hero with a special gift. This gift could be a map of the special world, an antidote to poison, or the key to a vault, or some other special magic needed for a successful quest. In many myths, the hero must pass a test to earn the gift. Great mentors possess the magic to influence their heroes in ways that are unique and will last a lifetime. Mentors are legitimate shortcuts to the treasure of your hero's journey.

The classic mentor is depicted in the 1950 Disney movie, Cinderella. Cinderella's fairy godmother not only fashions a beautiful ballroom gown and a pumpkin-shaped carriage but of course, the glass slippers. And don't forget those cute little mice that became horses to draw her carriage. We can all come up with plenty of classic mentors from contemporary movies. Dorothy collected mentors along the yellow brick road to her ultimate mentor— the wizard. In The Lord of the Rings, the mighty wizard Gandalf mentored Frodo. The grand teacher and wizard professor in the Harry Potter series, Dumbledore, mentored Harry Potter. Perhaps the most well-known mentor is the little green Jedi known as Yoda. Even though he is small, bald, has big hairy ears, and talks funny, he commands great respect. The way Yoda speaks forces us to pay attention and listen to his advice. When Luke says he can't believe it, Yoda's response is, "That is why you fail."

Through the years, I've hired many therapists and coaches to help me move through the times in my life when I was stuck or to help boost my businesses. But I've also gleaned a great deal of wisdom from books or seminars I've attended to aid me on my journeys, including the late great Wayne Dyer. I remember watching him on PBS as he talked about connecting with our source or Universe/God/Creator for inspiration and guidance.

I also found Tony Robbins—now considered the father of life coaching—early in his career as a life coach. I remember attending his seminars and listening to his cassette tapes on my lunch break in my car on cold winter days. Dr. Alex Loyd, Dr. Joe Dispenza, Ken Page, and Carol Pearson have also had enormous impacts on how I ultimately healed myself and began living my authentic life. Without mentors to teach and guide me, I would never have had the awareness needed to prepare for my journey. I want to also acknowledge all of the romantic partners in my life whom I've loved deeply and learned so much from. I believe that romantic relationships can be a doctorate degree in knowing yourself. Nothing allows us to learn about ourselves better than when we are suffering through a relationship breakup.

While I am on the topic of mentors, I would be remiss if I didn't plug my current profession of life coaching. Highly successful people know they didn't make it to the top by themselves. They all had coaches and mentors, but don't believe for a second that coaches and mentors are just for big shots. Hundreds of thousands of people participate in this time-honored tradition. No matter where you came from or where you are right now, you can also benefit from a good coach or mentor.

Let the Soul Journey Begin

From our ordinary world, we have heard, refused, and finally answered the call and gathered mentors. We have identified that the ego has developed and is prepared for the next phase of the hero's journey.

Now that we are prepared, the next phase is to venture into the unknown and find the soul. The ego sometimes gets a bad rap as being one of the main roadblocks to finding the soul. It is the ability of the ego to create and maintain boundaries. When the ego is properly developed, it can become the container for the soul. It becomes a safe place for the soul to connect with a person's spiritual vision.

This explains why people sometimes refuse the call for so long—they aren't ready yet. The ego has not learned its lessons yet. The ego needs to move through its healthy stages and be a place for the soul to rest and feel comfortable enough for the person to have the courage to take their journey. Sadly, though, most egos remain primitive and stuck, which does not allow the soul to flourish and come to life.

One of the problems is that the ego, an entity that was never meant to lead, sometimes gets out of control and highjacks one's psyche (all of our psychic processes including the conscious and subconscious). The ego is meant to be in the service of the soul and self. A healthy ego plays the intermediary for the whole self, while not thinking it is the whole self.

Is Your Ego Prepared for the Journey?

One of the ways you might recognize that you're not ready for the journey is when you find yourself continuously doing things so others will like you or think you are okay. Other signs you are not prepared include being unable to delegate, feeling you must run everything by yourself; being afraid to say what you think because someone might get angry; or being afraid to leave a relationship or a job for fear that you can't make it on your own. Or you may realize that you are taking care of everyone in your family or office except yourself. None of these issues indicate character flaws or insurmountable obstacles. They merely indicate that you haven't fully completed the developmental tasks of learning to trust in yourself and to stand up for yourself (autonomy). Therefore, the preparation for the journey almost always starts with the ego. Most of us have work to do to prepare for the deeper and more demanding elements of the journey. Remember that establishing a well-balanced ego is not being egotistical or selfish. You will still care about others, but you must trust yourself to take a stand for yourself and others.

The simplest way to deal with the underdeveloped ego's fear of change is to observe it with detachment. Before we can take our hero's journey, the ego needs to agree to come along because it is the practical, down-to-earth part that sees to it that our journeys do not spin our lives out of control.

One of the most powerful experiences I have ever had on my hero's journey was the first time I was able to detach from my ego. A few years after my divorce, I was having a particularly hard time accepting a difficult relationship breakup. I remember feeling this surge of rage come over me and I did not know how to deal with it. I decided I needed to burn off some energy, so I got on my bike and tore down the road. I pedaled harder than I had in years and was exhausted and sweaty and tired. I pulled my bike to the side of the trail to rest, when suddenly, I had this vision of a tiny little man throwing a tantrum, screaming and yelling, and being extremely foolish. I instantly identified this as my ego. I saw this crazy ego off to the side of me which revealed a pure white area in my chest that I also instantly identified as my soul. I had, for the first time ever, detached my ego from my soul and could see that my soul was pure white, and glowing, and innocent, and calm. I began to connect with my glowing soul and my heart rate came down. I felt the most at peace in that moment than I had in a long, long time.

Being able to detach and see my ego as separate from me was key. It gave me a sense of freedom that I had been searching for. For the first time, I could deeply feel that I was no longer trapped by my ego's rigid dependency on maintaining control and needing to please everyone. One of the areas where my ego was undeveloped was in not trusting myself. I felt I always had to become someone I wasn't to please people. Detaching my ego and seeing my beautiful soul freed me to love my soul, and ultimately, myself.

EXERCISE 1
YOUR LIFE TIMELINE

Complete a timeline of your life up until now. List the most significant events. This isn't a detailed list of your whole life, but it will give you a good idea of where you are in the twelve stages of the hero's journey exercise below.

Example Timeline

Year	Life Event
1962	Born in Helena, Montana
1980	Graduated from Flathead High School
1986	Graduated from University of Montana with a psychology degree
1987	Packed up my Honda Civic and drove across the country to start my life in Washington, DC
1987	Got my first real job at Tymnet—living in Northern Virginia
1989	Got married
...	...

Your Turn:

Year	Life Event

EXERCISE 2
PREPARATION PHASE

Reread the first four stages of the Preparation phase of the hero's journey. Then place your life events into each stage. Make sure to identify not only what was going on in your life at this time but what this time in your life meant to you. Don't worry if you can't identify a part of your life that doesn't fit into a particular stage. You can skip it or come back to it later.

Decide as early in the process as you can if you are going to list out your entire life until now into one big hero's journey or you think you may have had more than one already. Remember that you can have multiple events in your life that may be in one stage. For example, you may have had many calls to adventure but refused the call many times before actually crossing the threshold. I find it helpful to try and fit a large chunk of life into one hero's journey. You may, and usually will, find that you are in the middle of your hero's journey with a few stages yet to move through.

Stage One: The Ordinary World

Try to remember a time in your life when you were living your life and seemingly things were fine, but you felt a small inkling that something wasn't quite right and there was something more out there for you. Detail the date and time in your life and describe what was going on in your life then.

Example:

I was living in suburbia with my two kids and my wife. I was working my ass off to get ahead and make a good life for my family. I wasn't exercising or eating a good diet, and I was becoming miserable. I began to think something in my life had to change.

Your Turn:

_____

_____

_____

Stage Two: The Call to Adventure

Now that you have established your ordinary world, follow through your timeline to when something happened in your life that woke you up and got your attention. This could be a hardship like a job loss, divorce, or loss of a loved one, or it could be that you just woke up one day and knew you had to make a change in your life.

Example:

I was in the shower when I heard a voice say, "This is not the way to live your life—you must be doing something wrong."

Your Turn:

_____

_____

_____

Stage Three: Refusal of the Call

Describe a time in your life when you heard the call to adventure but were too afraid or confused to follow through and make a change in your life.

Example:

I repeatedly refused the call. After I heard the call in the shower that morning it would be another nine years before I would fully answer the call, enter my new world by getting a divorce, leaving a job of 16 years, and starting my own business.

Your Turn:

Stage Four: Meeting with the Mentor

Who has been a mentor to you in your life? Mentors can be people you admired or learned from either before your call to adventure or after. As you progress through your journey you may lean on these mentors heavily or acquire new ones.

Example:

Through the years, I've hired many therapists and coaches to help me move through the stuck times in life or to help boost my businesses. I've also gleaned a great deal of wisdom from books or seminars I have attended to aid me on my journey.

Your Turn:

EXERCISE 3
IS YOUR EGO PREPARED
FOR THE JOURNEY?

The following questions will help you determine what Preparation stage you need help with or what events should fit into a certain stage.

- What calls for change are presenting themselves to you right now?

_____

- Are there calls from your past that you have ignored or refused? Do they still call out to you?

_____

- To whom did you look for direction when you were growing up?

_____

- Are there others who acted directly or indirectly as teachers or coaches?

_____

- Would life be different if you hadn't met your mentors?

_____

Now that you have completed your Preparation phase stages, answer the following questions to help you decide if your ego has progressed in a developmentally healthy way. Don't be critical if you still need work in this area. Most of us do.

- Do you find yourself continuously doing things so others will like you or think you are okay?

_____

- Do you have a hard time delegating? Do you feel you must run everything by yourself?

_____

- Do you have a hard time accepting other people's wishes or truths even if they conflict with yours?

_____

- Are you afraid to say what you think because someone might get angry, or are you afraid to leave a relationship or a job for fear that you can't make it on your own?

_____

- Do you have a hard time accepting constructive criticism?

_____

- Are you taking care of everyone in your family or office except yourself?

_____

These answers should allow you to pinpoint areas that you may need to continue to work on before or as you move into the Journey and Return phases. They may also show you areas that you might want to change or add to your above stages.

CHAPTER 4
PHASE II – THE JOURNEY

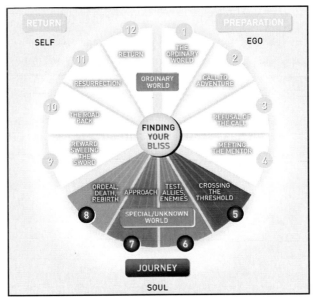

THE HERO'S JOURNEY MAP

In the second phase of the hero's journey, we finally step across the threshold into the special world and start looking at our subconscious mind. The journey requires us to see the truth of the soul, which doesn't necessarily make sense to the rational ego, but it's what makes us feel alive and real by journeying into the mysteries of life where we learn about life and death, intimacy, sex, passion, mystery, spirit, and the things the soul craves. Without the soul, we feel like machines just going through the motions. Sometimes we ignore the experiences of the journey because we are so out of

touch with our souls that we are unaffected and untransformed—
we have our blinders on. But make no mistake, it's never too late
to cross the threshold and take our hero's journey. The only down-
side to failing to take the soul's journey is the ever-present sense
of emptiness and meaninglessness—which is punishment enough.

Once we answer the call and cross the threshold, we step into the
soul's inner world. This is the soul's initiation process. It shakes up
one's way of seeing the world and requires that a person connect
with deeper wisdom to understand what is happening. As you
will see in the following stages, initiation may in some ways be
painful. You may experience suffering, confusion, and loss, but it
is, of course, this initiation that finally allows for the birth of the
new self. This phase is also about what Campbell called "following
your bliss." As your journey progresses, the essence of the hero's
journey is in finding and following that bliss—your life's purpose
and your "big why." As the Sufi mystic Rumi said, "Let yourself be
silently drawn by the strange pull of what you really love. It will
not lead you astray."

Knowing yourself well prepares you when life in the Journey phase
presents sharp turns and rocky roads. This will help you avoid being derailed by irrelevant chaos and noise. You'll know what you
value, what's important, and why. This also allows you to make
timely decisions, enhance your well-being, and make the world a
better place.

For example, in the *Rocky* movie series, Rocky, played by Syl-
vester Stallone, goes through his ups and downs, fighting and
training, and losing and then winning, and then losing again. He
learns to know himself. In the sixth movie in the series, *Rocky
Balboa,* Rocky is confronted by his son, who doesn't want him
to fight again. Rocky tells his son that "it's not about how hard
you can hit, it's about how hard you get hit and keep moving
forward. That's how winning is done."

What Is Your Purpose

Recognizing your passions and landing on your purpose is where your power lies. Unfortunately, your purpose won't flash before your eyes in a "the future is so bright" moment. It's usually a slow burn that ignites a knowing and peacefulness as you come to understand your purpose and figure out your big why. The tests and trials of this phase will help forge your values and beliefs, and ultimately lead to your purpose.

Normal, everyday activities like taking care of your family do not help identify your specific purpose. Of course, these are worthy activities, but they could apply to just about anyone. You need to uncover what your specific purpose is. Find where your power lies and what is unique about you that stands out and makes a difference in other people's lives. What is it that you do better than most people? Take time to get quiet, write in a journal, and contemplate these questions and I promise you will find your purpose. There are some great exercises that appear later in this book that will help you identify your purpose.

On some level, you know you are a hero. When you find your purpose, it's like finding your superhero powers. What are your superpowers? You might not know until you fight some internal battles.

Don't get me wrong, finding your bliss and purpose is hard. It's through the battles that you'll find the answers to the burning questions you asked above. However, once you find it, it won't be all smooth sailing as doubts and fears of failure will creep up on you. But having a purpose allows you to focus on your future and choose your battles wisely.

My client, H.O., had been writing most of her life but had never published anything other than a few newspaper articles. She even led a writer's retreat once a year that helped other authors get their books published. H.O. never believed she could become a paid author. She gave up her idea of being a successful author years ago when she decided to give all her attention to her family. As we worked through her hero's journey she realized where she had given up on her passion of writing professionally. As we searched for her bliss she started to realize that she loves being a mom and that her friends always told her how funny she was. From this understanding she started a very successful and humorous blog aimed at mothers and women who take care of the household. She is now finally writing the book she always wanted to write and plans to publish it next year.

When you find your purpose, life flows effortlessly, you're in your power zone, and you find it all exhilarating and fulfilling. Chances are, you will be drawn to helping others thrive. It's a win-win situation. Often, purpose and passion can be very similar and almost seem to be one. Purpose tends to be the reason you're on your hero's journey (the why), while passion lights your way. Follow your passions vigorously and you'll eventually find purpose and the real hero's journey treasure.

Stage Five: Crossing the Threshold—Pursue Your Purpose

In stories and movies, this is the end of Act One. The hero commits to leaving the ordinary world and enters a new region or condition with unfamiliar rules and values.

Crossing the threshold is when we finally answer the call and step out into the unknown. It's the scariest thing we've ever had to face but it's our time and we take that leap.

According to Campbell, once we hear the call and are willing to take on the challenges of that newly awakened life, we begin to feel a powerful energy come over us. We wake up seeing that we are the heroes of our own lives and are tired of being victims. Campbell also talks about a metaphorical death where something dies, so something else can live. And in every hero's journey, there is some death moment where something old must go and something new is born.

In myth, when someone dies, it doesn't just mean the end of a biological life. It's an indication that change is taking place. Without death, there is no transformation. The key to recognizing death is that it's just one old pattern that has played itself out and is of no use to us anymore. Like the phoenix, one rises again in some new form that has new intrinsic meaning and makes life even better.

In the 1999 movie, *The Matrix,* we see Neo, played by Keanu Reeves, sitting in a plush leather chair. He is presented with a choice. In the now famous scene, Morpheus, played by Laurence Fishburne, says to Neo, "You take the blue pill, the story ends, you wake up in your bed and believe whatever you want to believe. You take the red pill, you stay in Wonderland and I show you how deep the rabbit hole goes." As Neo contemplates whether to cross the threshold, he is cautioned that if he takes the red pill, there is no turning back. This is the essence of the decision we must all make as the Universe/God/Creator calls us to our journey.

My initial crossing-the-threshold moment came after I said to hell with all the doctors and physical therapists. At that point, I wasn't sure what to do other than try to chill out. For someone who had been anxious, stressed out, and in pain for a long time, this proved to be a lot harder than it sounded. I started to take Tai Chi and yoga classes, and started reading about how to reduce stress. It was very slow going and I vacillated between answering the call and refusing the call. I finally entered my new world by getting a divorce and leaving a job I had held for 16 years. All in one year! Now, that's a lot of metaphorical death. But those parts needed to go so I could find the parts that could stay and grow and be healthy, both physically and mentally.

Stage Six: Tests, Allies, and Enemies—How You May Be Helped or Sabotaged

Once a hero finally gets the courage to jump, the hero is tested, finds allies, and learns the rules of the special world. The hero needs to discover who can be trusted. A sidekick may join, or an entire hero team can be forged. It's unknown because we have entered a place where we have always been too afraid to go. The hero must prepare for the greater ordeals to come and needs this stage to test skills and powers, or perhaps seek further training from the mentor. This initiation into the special world also tests the hero's commitment to the journey, and questions whether they can succeed.

Like all mythological heroes, Hercules and Achilles received their share of great strength and skills while facing increasingly difficult challenges. This isn't so different in our lives as we are constantly bettering our skills and becoming stronger with each new challenge. We are truly the heroes of our lives.

In the sixth stage, friends and allies will be drawn to your aid but allies must be earned. It's important to attract as many quality allies as we can to support us through the journey of the soul.

In the 1993 movie, *Schindler's List,* Oskar Schindler, played by Liam Neeson, was a classic hero who aligned himself with Jewish allies to help him rebuild an old Polish factory to make pots and pans to sell to the German army. His main ally was Itzhak Stern, played by Ben Kingsley, a Jewish accountant Schindler hired as his right-hand man to recruit Jewish laborers and run his business. The Jewish workers were also his allies as they worked hard so the factory would seem valuable to the Nazis. They kept the factory open and continued to use Jewish workers, who were given a haven if they worked in Schindler's factory.

Schindler's tests came in making an effort to keep the factory open, and by extension, keeping his workers out of the death camps. On many occasions, Schindler would give his personal items to his workers to use as trade currency. Clearly, he had a conscience and did what he could to save as many Jewish people as possible. In the end, Schindler paid to move more than 800 Jewish workers to Hungary, where they would eventually escape and be set free.

As for the enemy? It was the Nazi army machine itself and the evil Commandant Amon Goeth, played by Ralph Fiennes. He was pure evil as he would leisurely gun down Jewish people as they walked down the streets.

There will always be enemies that stand in the way of moving forward in our journey and in a metaphorical way we must defeat them so we can fulfill our destiny. Enemies, of course, don't always have to be other people. They can sometimes be the internal enemies of self-doubt and negative self-talk that we must overcome.

After my divorce, I started a new career as a professional portrait photographer. Now that all my old familiar friends from the marriage and my work were gone, I had to meet new friends and make new allies. I met a particularly interesting woman and business coach in the office where my new photography studio was located. I hired her to consult with me in business. She treated me like we were long lost friends. She was very professional and had very positive energy. She was extremely nice. To be honest, at first, I thought she was interested in me as more than just a client. Then one day, I saw her interacting with other people in the office and realized that was how she treated everyone. I asked her why she was so friendly, and she said she just treats everyone she meets like she knows them already, and her positive energy and enthusiasm just comes out. She eventually became one of my trusted friends and allies as we created the first one-of-a-kind (as we knew it) energy club. We would go from place to place and try to find like-minded positive energy nuts and recruit them into our club.

Of course, our meetings were always held in bars, but this eventually turned into a business for her, and I became the official photographer. Meeting her and starting the energy club was my first initiation into understanding the power of a positive attitude, appreciating good energy, spreading the love wherever you go, and surrounding yourself with positive people. This was a powerful introduction to the notion that strong friend relationships are key to a happy and healthy life.

My photography business morphed into a video and internet marketing consulting business, and I was working out of coffee shops and meeting new and interesting people. I found kindred souls and fellow entrepreneurs and formed strong friendships that have lasted to this day. One thing I learned during this time was how the Universe/God/Creator is always supporting you if you just settle the mind and let the innate intelligence come through and work its magic. The relationships I was forming in this new period of my life would become crucial in the final painful stages of my journey. This time in my life wasn't without tests and trials, though. I had worked in the corporate world all my adult life and was not nearly ready for entrepreneurship. Corporate life is completely different than being an entrepreneur, and I struggled to keep up with honing my technical skills, marketing my business, and dealing with all the new tax and insurance issues unique to entrepreneurs. Thankfully, I had befriended other entrepreneurs and we helped each other through the struggles.

Stage Seven: The Approach—Nearing the Target and Second Guessing Your Purpose

In the seventh stage, the call has been answered and the hero and newfound allies prepare for the major challenge in the special world. We know what must be done and we prepare for it. Meetings are held, preparations are made, and practice sessions commence.

The 2001 movie, *Ocean's Eleven,* was about the approach. Director Stephen Soderbergh set out to remake the 1960 Rat Pack version of this movie. It starred an ensemble cast including George Clooney, Brad Pitt, Matt Damon, and Julia Roberts.

Immediately after Danny Ocean gets out of jail, he plots to rob three Las Vegas casinos at once. He rallies his gang (allies) together and begins to plan for the heist.

The movie unfolds in a fun way, wherein we learn of the plan by watching it unfold in real time. Of course, our hero, Danny, gets the money and the girl at the end.

Planning and preparing is important as we move into uncharted territory. This is a time to study and learn about ourselves. To assess our strengths and weaknesses and prepare for what lies ahead. As in the movie, we need to gather our resources for what lies ahead.

As my consulting business was taking off, I started to focus on my body and began eating healthier and exercising more. I even went on a grain-free diet and lost 40 pounds. I dated on and off, but found I was very rusty after 19 years of marriage and therefore didn't have much success in those early years. I started to devour my mentor's content and started practicing Qigong, meditation, and mindfulness.

Meditation is not easy at first. It takes commitment to keep doing it, despite your mind going crazy with every miscellaneous thought it can find. As I stuck with it, I began to see a gradual change in my awareness and presence. I learned about mindfulness, and it became my quest to live a mindful life. This is where I started to look inside for answers and understand how my subconscious was primarily ruling my life.

Stage Eight: The Ordeal—Taking a Leap of Faith and Dying to Be Reborn

Near the middle of the story, the hero enters a central space in the special world where they confront death or face their greatest fear. Out of the moment of death comes a new life, but the journey often teeters on the brink of failure. This is where the hero faces personal demons and battles fears. It's scary and hard. During this stage, we may feel like we've been defeated for a while. But out of defeat comes victory. Remember, this is *your* inner journey and you are in control. Things you feared in the past are just unknowns. If you seek to understand them, you are on the path to your treasure.

Unfortunately, you can't prepare for what your exact ordeal will be. You will probably have to take a leap of faith. This is where most refuse the call and back away. Leaping into the unknown takes courage and it will take you way out of your comfort zone. To overcome fear, the hero relies on skills and training gathered from earlier stages of the journey. We must metaphorically cut off pieces of ourselves that are holding us back from being our hero.

The hero must sacrifice and die to be reborn. Something must be given up, such as an old habit, or outdated belief—we must come to terms with our shortcomings. The ordeal is the turning point after which everything is changed and the hero can never go back.

The "dark night of the soul" is a term used to describe the dismantling of a perceived meaning of life. It's when we give up our preconceived notions of who we are and how we behave in life that triggers a major reset. This metaphorical rebooting can take days, weeks, or months, and living through it can be the scariest thing you have ever experienced. Unfortunately, the only way out is through it. You must accept it, trust it, and walk through it. If you back away, it will grow stronger. For the hero, this is the confrontation of the shadow self, the part of you that you don't want to admit, and the biggest casualty will likely be the ego. Our greatest fear is that we won't be able to live without it—and we're right. Only through the ego's death can we experience the resurrection that empowers us to fulfill our destiny.

At this stage, we are becoming aware that major change is taking place. Everything that has transpired during the journey comes to a head at the ordeal, and everything after it is about the return home. The death of the ego's stronghold opens a space for one to experience a rebirth and become the real hero of one's life.

In one of my favorite movie scenes of all time, *Star Wars: The Empire Strikes Back*, Luke Skywalker must face his greatest fear by entering the dark cave on the planet Dagobah as instructed by the Jedi Master, Yoda. As he enters the dark and dreary cave, he is confronted with snakes and creatures. He ignites his lightsaber to see better and we hear the familiar sound of Darth Vader's breathing. The two face off in a lightsaber battle where Luke finally chops off Darth Vader's head. As it falls to the ground, Luke sees that underneath the mask is his image. Luke has just faced, and metaphorically defeated, his greatest fear—that he would turn out to be evil like his father, Darth Vader.

The importance of the concept that something old in you must die for the new you to be reborn can't be emphasized enough. It is the essence of why we take our hero's journey.

In my experience, this stage was very long and painful. I have identified two parts of my life where I faced uphill battles and have named these my "dark days." After my life changed dramatically because of my divorce, leaving my job, and starting my own business, things were slowly looking up. I was enjoying my new freedom and was excited about my new business. I poured my heart and soul into it seven days a week. Unfortunately, I became lonely and frustrated with the slow growth of the business, and I started drinking a lot. It came on so slowly because I had never been a big drinker. I didn't drink at all while raising my kids, but I slowly built up a tolerance and was soon drinking every night with dinner and getting drunk at least one night a week. I started to put myself in dangerous situations by hanging out with a bad crowd. One night, I found myself at a Denny's in a part of the city I'd never been before. Armed guards flanked the entrance. I was hanging out with people I didn't know, and under normal circumstances, would never have been around. I was very lucky to find myself home in bed the next morning but didn't know exactly how I got there. I wish I could say this was when I hit bottom, but it wasn't. I would continue to drink and gamble for another two years, until I met another lost soul, a woman who needed someone as badly as I did. In our time together, we healed each other a bit and were both able to curb our drinking considerably.

But this time in my life still felt like the long dark night of the soul. I knew I had to cut this woman out of my life and start a new chapter. Unfortunately, the Universe/God/Creator wasn't done with me—my next chapter wasn't a pleasant one.

One winter day, I noticed a weird lump under my arm but was sure it was nothing because I was not experiencing any pain or symptoms. Finally, after ignoring it for three months, I decided to have my doctor check it out. She didn't seem too concerned but thought I should get a biopsy just in case. That's not what you want to hear, but I was still optimistic they would find a clogged duct or something and after some medication I'd be fine.

I waited over a week for the results and kept calling my doctor to see if there was any news, but she didn't know why it was taking so long. That's not good for anyone's stress level. I finally got the call everyone dreads. "Scott, you have cancer and the reason it took so long is that you have a rare form of lymphoma."

Wham! The Universe/God/Creator just knocked me on my ass again. Okay, so that's not good, I thought. But before I could get too caught up in my own grief and terror, I realized that my poor kids were now going to have both their parents in chemo at the same time and could lose us both. Yes, my ex-wife had breast cancer and had just started her chemotherapy sessions. It tore me up. It was harder to tell my children this than it had been to tell them we were getting divorced five years earlier.

This was no ordinary world. It was a crazy, scary new world filled with chemo, hair loss, radiation, and fear. Thank God I had already crossed the threshold, entered my hero's journey, and was preparing. I was lucky to catch my cancer at Stage 1. Cancer therapy these days has come a long way, and although I lost my hair and was weak at times, I was able to carry on my work and most of my daily activities during treatment.

You would think that having cancer and going through treatment would be the worst thing that could happen to someone. But in my case, I realized that my first health crises with my stomach and back, and subsequently climbing out of it prepared me for dealing with cancer. Once I knew we caught it at Stage 1, I just knew everything was going to be all right. I just tried to be as happy and positive as I could. I chatted up every nurse, doctor, and hospital food handler I could find. I feel that my positive attitude helped me cope with my life-threatening situation. The take away after finishing my treatment and being cancer free at the end of that year was realizing how being on my journey and being aware and mindful helped with my relatively easy bout with cancer.

Is Your Soul Prepared for the Return?

The Journey phase is the time to examine your life and ask the tough questions. The journey is a time to let go of control of your life and ask questions, challenge the status quo, and take responsibility for who you are and the person you want to become. You must ask, what is my true purpose in life? What changes must I make? How can I best use my gifts and talents? What can I believe in? To do this you must let go of safety and predictably. By doing so you move out of the world of good or bad, me or you, us or them, light or dark, and into a world of paradox. If you have prepared well, you will have allowed your ego to let go of a perfect world where everything makes sense. Don't worry, the journey of the soul doesn't mean that any sense of control is gone forever. Once you finish your hero's journey and reconcile with the self in the Return phase, life will feel whole and on point.

EXERCISE 4
THE JOURNEY

Stage Five: Crossing the Threshold

Review your timeline and find the time in your life where you finally said, enough with this old way of thinking or living! and actually made a change in your life. You were finally able to move out of your comfort zone and start something new or end something that needed ending, and it changed your life in a new direction. If you can't think of a time when you feel you've crossed the threshold, then maybe you are still refusing the call in your ordinary life. That's okay. Try and imagine a future timeline for your hero's journey and use it as a catalyst to move forward in your life.

Example:

My initial crossing the threshold came after I said to hell with all the doctors and physical therapists. At this point, I wasn't sure what to do other than try to chill out.

Your Turn:

_____

_____

_____

Stage Six: Tests, Allies, and Enemies

Now that you've crossed the threshold and are living in the new, unfamiliar, special world, identify any trials and tribulations you went through as you moved through this new and unfamiliar territory. List friends and allies that appeared during this time who helped you get through them. Also list or describe any enemies that you needed to face down. Enemies can also be difficult situations that you had to overcome.

Example:

After my divorce I started a new career as a professional portrait photographer. Now that all my old familiar friends from the marriage and my work were gone, I had to go out and meet new friends and make new allies.

Your Turn:

_____

_____

_____

Stage Seven: The Approach

Define a time in your life when you went into planning or strengthening or learning mode. This is a time in your life where you were in the thick of life. You are living in the new world and preparing to grow stronger—physically, emotionally, or both. You may not have known it at the time but you were preparing for even harder times ahead. This can be a very good time in your life when you felt like you were alive because you were moving forward.

Example:

As my consulting business was taking off, I started to focus on my body, and I began eating healthier and exercising more. I even went on a grain-free diet and lost 40 pounds.

Your Turn:

_____

_____

_____

Stage Eight: The Ordeal

Describe a time in your life where you had to face a situation scarier than anything you had encountered before. Detail what it was, what you went through, and the insights it brought. There may be more than one ordeal that comes to mind. Just pick one at this time that fits with your timeline and hero's journey so far. There will be other times in your journey where you will undergo trials and tribulations and have to face dragons and ogres, and you can list them then.

Example:

This stage for me was very long and painful. I have identified two parts of my life where I faced uphill battles and have named these my "dark days."

Your Turn:

_____

_____

_____

EXERCISE 5
IS YOUR SOUL PREPARED FOR THE RETURN?

Now that you have completed the Journey phase, it is time to reflect. Remember times when you felt satisfied or curious or content and allowed yourself to be fully present with all the sensations and images that fed your desires. As you build momentum along your journey, you can also allow your fantasies to soar. Ask the following questions of yourself gently and repeat each question or answer each prompt until you are satisfied with your answer. For example: "I like _____. Another thing I like is _____." Don't edit or critique your answers. Answer each question with the first words that pop into your head.

- I like _____.
- I feel satisfied when _____.
- I fully enjoy _____.
- I want to do more _____.
- I am happy when I _____.
- What dreams do I have, day or night, that reveal my purpose? _____ _____.
- I feel fulfilled when I _____.
- I feel curious about_____.
- If I could change anything in my life I would change _____.

- In my wildest fantasies, I have always wanted to ____
  _____.

- My gifts, talents, and strengths include _____
  _____.

Now, review your list and decide which of these you can pass on to others.

- Of all my gifts, talents, and strengths, which is my best, the one that makes me stand out?
  _____.

- Am I willing to give up the life I've planned so I can have the life that is waiting for me?
  _____.

- Where in my life am I playing defense? What would it look like to play some offense?
  _____.

- One thing that I will do today that scares me is ___
  _____.

These answers should allow you to pinpoint areas that you may need to continue to work on before you can move into the Return phase.

CHAPTER 5
PHASE III — THE RETURN

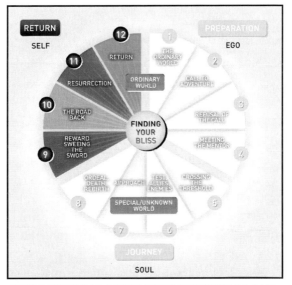

THE HERO'S JOURNEY RETURN MAP

In the final phase of the hero's journey, one explores the self, which is an expression of wholeness and the endpoint in the process. The journey has been completed, the treasure gained, and the kingdom—one's life—has been transformed. Hitting the reset button all seems worth it now that the ordeal is over. The self is the entry point into a whole new way of living; moving one out of "life as a struggle" and into abundance. The journey is ending when one realizes the fruits of the ordeal by finding their bliss—one's authentic true self and purpose. The hero starts acting on newfound thoughts and ideas and begins to tell their story. Being conscious involves waking up and taking a new kind of responsibility for one's life; becoming a true, authentic, and productive member of the human race.

In the final phase of the hero's journey, we are finally able to express ourselves in the world. But no integration of consciousness lasts forever, and sooner or later that consciousness will split and the journey will begin again.

We have been through the Preparation and Journey phases, and we now enter the final phase of self-renewal. The transition from change to renewal is life changing.

The goal of the outward journey is a visible achievement—reaching a destination or winning a battle. The purpose of the inner journey is internal fulfillment and self-actualization. While the inciting incident, the call to adventure, triggers the outward quest; it is an incessant call from within that provokes heroes to achieve their destiny. In the classic definition, a hero is someone who gives their life to something bigger than themself. The journey is of initiation—of awakening an inner power of spiritual knowing. Facing both external and internal obstacles, the hero confronts fears, as well as external challenges to ensure survival. Conquering the forces rallied against them, heroes emerge as their authentic selves—victorious and empowered.

Bringing subconscious limiting beliefs into the light of consciousness is great, but once we realize our subconscious beliefs are in control, we must identify the culprits. Pushing through the rest of the block requires us to be accountable for our commitments. When we say we're going to do something and are true to our word, motivation improves and our commitment gets stronger. We can stay on track and move forward. Accountability enables us to commit to getting results.

Stage Nine: The Reward—The Treasure Is Found

At the end of the hero's journey, the hero takes possession of the treasure. There may be a celebration, but there is also danger of losing the treasure again.

As the hero of your journey, you took the bull by the horns and transformed misfortune into fortune. You wouldn't be the same person today without the misfortunes you have endured. Most of us will do anything to avoid misfortune, but we need not run from it. It is our responsibility to transform misfortune into our treasure.

The Godfather, which debuted in 1972, is widely regarded as one of the best movies of all time. It depicts the powerful Italian-American crime family of Don Vito Corleone, played brilliantly by Marlon Brando. The don's youngest son, Michael, played by Al Pacino, reluctantly joins the family business after his father's death but ultimately takes on the mantle of leadership. In a full-out power grab, Michael has all the other heads of the New York mafia killed. In the end, Michael celebrates his victory by having his men kiss his hand to show their loyalty. He is the new Godfather now. Just as in any good hero's journey movie, this only marks the beginning of danger ahead, as depicted in *The Godfather Part II* and *The Godfather Part III* where Michael faces even harsher enemies and consequences to his actions.

We have all experienced the bittersweet feeling of claiming victory one moment just to have it all snatched away the next. My victory was being declared cancer free after a year of treatment. I had conquered my fearful ordeal and won the battle. I was back on track, living my life, and consulting in Kansas. I had moved into a new apartment, started a new area of consulting in internet marketing, and wrote my second book called Monetize Your Message. It was a book on how to create online courses and sell them on the internet. I was happy and trying to get my strength back, and wanting to get back in the dating pool again, since my hair had grown back and I had lost a few pounds. Little did I know that the next phase of my journey would entail even more pain and suffering, this time emotional, but ultimately lead to an enlightenment that would change the course of my life yet again and prepare me for my return.

Stage Ten: The Road Back—Danger and Problems Keeping the Treasure

About three-fourths of the way through the hero's journey in the movies, the hero is driven to complete the adventure, leaving the special world to bring the treasure home. Often, a chase scene signals the urgency and danger of the mission. This is a critical stage because no matter what the victory, the hero must complete the journey and bring back the treasure. This is where a lot of us falter. We take our eye off the ball and we fumble.

The road home is fraught with peril. In the 1981 movie, *Raiders of The Lost Ark*, Indiana Jones, played by Harrison Ford, encounters many obstacles. Most of the movie shows the perilous road back for Indiana after he finds the lost treasure of the ark of the covenant.

Just as he finds the ark in an underground cavern in Cairo, the Nazi army, who also wants the ark, traps Indiana in the cavern and takes the ark. Of course, a dark cave filled with snakes is no match for Indiana Jones. After he escapes the cavern, he steals a horse, finds the Nazi caravan carrying the ark, and manages to highjack a truck and get the ark onto a ship to transport back to the United States.

But the hero's road back is challenging. The Nazis catch him in a submarine and steal the ark back again. Before they present the ark to Hitler, the Nazis decide to open it to make sure it contains the treasure inside. This turns out to be a big mistake. When they open the ark it spews torrents of flames that kill all the Nazis. Indiana is unhurt by the flames because he keeps his eyes shut. He finally brings the treasure home where the US government confiscates the ark for their own research.

My client, H.O., faced a hard road back after overcoming her challenges as well. She had just finished working very hard to get her family out of debt. Her husband resented her controlling their finances and threatened to do what he wanted with his money, implying that since he was the main breadwinner in the family he should be allowed to spend money as he saw fit. For H.O. the return to a holistic and happy family was threatened by her husband's spendthrift ways and it threatened to derail their 30-year marriage.

In my life, when I reached the tenth stage, the only chase scene I was experiencing was my dating failures. I was chasing my tail trying to find true love again. I tried various ways to find my soulmate—from meetups, to online dating, to hanging out in bars—with no success. I was beginning to feel discouraged, like I may have dropped the ball on my journey and I was stuck again. After my divorce six years earlier, I figured my life would be further along, but I was still single and living in an apartment.

Stage Eleven: The Resurrection—Overcoming the Final Demons

After the climax, in a typical story of a hero's journey, the hero is severely tested once more on the threshold of home. He or she is purified by a last sacrifice—another moment of death and rebirth—but on a higher and more complete level. By the hero's actions, the polarities that were in conflict at the beginning are being resolved.

The Resurrection stage is probably the most difficult stage for us. We are so close. We are happy that we've made so much progress, and we're celebrating on the road home when the most severe test yet knocks us on our asses. But here's the key. At this point, we've already been through a lot. We have moved through the stages of healthy ego development and taken our soul journey, faced dragons and ogres, and gained friends and mentors. We are as healthy and emotionally evolved as we have ever been. We've gained knowledge and power that we didn't know was possible. So even though this is a huge test, we are ready for it. And finally, after this purifying event, those polarities that have been plaguing us most of our lives have finally been put to rest.

The resurrection may be a physical ordeal or final showdown between the hero and the shadow. This battle is for much more than the hero's life. Other lives, or an entire world, may be at stake, and the hero must now prove that they have achieved heroic status and willingly accept their sacrifice for the benefit of the ordinary world. Other allies may come to the rescue at the last minute to lend assistance, but in the end, the hero must rise to the sacrifice at hand. They must deliver the final blow and accept the "magic elixir."

This scenario plays out in the 1995 smash hit, *Toy Story*, directed by John Lasseter. The hero of our story, Woody, gets himself into a bit of a pickle. Because he is jealous of his owner Andy's new toy, Buzz Lightyear, he inadvertently knocks Buzz out of the window and Buzz lands in the backyard of the evil, toy-destroying boy named Sid.

While attempting to rescue Buzz from Sid, Woody ends up in Sid's room with Buzz, and both are faced with their apparent doom. Woody's resurrection comes when he has a chance to escape on his own but decides he can't leave Buzz behind. He convinces Sid's maimed toys to help by coming to life in front of Sid and scaring the crap out of him. Both Woody and Buzz escape and rush to catch the moving van taking Andy's family to a new house. Andy's other toys come to their rescue and help them get back to Andy's new room where they can live their lives with Andy and his family.

The resurrection part of my story is critical because it was the catalyst to my healing, writing this book, and starting my life coaching career. Remember, everyone's hero's journey is personal, and for some, the call to adventure, the ordeal, or the resurrection is a love loss. I had been dating on and off since returning to Kansas, but nothing was even remotely serious. One day, out of the blue, I met a woman I would eventually fall in love with and who profoundly changed the course of my life.

We dated on and off for a year. When our relationship ended I took it pretty hard. During a particularly painful "off" period in our relationship, I was digging deep inside to figure out why I was suffering so much. I kept telling myself that breakups happen all the time, and I asked myself why this one was so painful for me. I had many relationships come and go and was married for 19 years, but nothing came close to the suffering I was feeling after this breakup. Luckily, I was in the Return phase of my journey and I had accumulated mystical powers and trusted allies. My mystical power turned out to be the ability to see that the answer to my suffering was within me, not outside. Something inside me had been triggered, and some deep feeling was activated and needed to be heard. I began to read about the Buddhist approach to suffering and learned the concept of the Four Noble Truths of suffering— suffering itself, the cause of suffering, the end of suffering, and the path that leads to ending suffering. It's a doctrine that essentially says that suffering exists and arises from attachment to desires and ceases when attachment to desire ceases. You see, I had created a fantasy in my head about me and my partner, and I became so attached to that fantasy that the reality of the situation didn't seem to matter. When I understood this, I could see that I was in love with the fantasy more than I was with her. I began to journal daily about my suffering to make sense of it. I began to see that my subconscious was being triggered.

The opening that was created started to expand and I found there were other areas of my life that needed work. I began to examine my work life and began to figure out if I was doing what I truly loved to do, and if I was "living in my bliss," as Joseph Campbell would say. Part of that path came with getting out of my head and into my heart and helping people. I began to volunteer with local nonprofits and give away my time and talents to help them and others. It felt good to help others—it is one of life's most powerful healing elixirs. Just as Campbell states that part of the Resurrection is a fight for more than just the hero, I started a blog called Be the Change You Want that highlighted people working together to solve the nation's problems, instead of being so divisive. I realized that I wanted to help others who were stuck in their lives and needed a way to understand themselves better. I wanted to help them find their true mission and live a fulfilling life. I also had a few dear friends (allies) who stood with me during my suffering and didn't try to fix me; they just listened with acknowledgment and grace.

If you are at this stage but still don't seem to know what your passion is or your gifts to the world are, try looking at your suffering. Diving deep to figure out the source of your suffering will illuminate your greatest gifts. It worked for me and I know it will work for you too.

Stage Twelve: Return with the Elixir/Treasure—Your Purpose Is Fulfilled

Returning with the treasure is the final reward that is earned on the hero's journey. The hero has been resurrected and purified, and has earned the right to be accepted back into the ordinary world and share the treasure of the journey. The true hero returns with treasure to share with others or heal a wounded land. The treasure can be great wealth or a magic potion. It can also be love, wisdom, or simply the experience of having survived the special world. These treasures allow the hero to return to the ordinary conscious world and share valuable insights and perspectives and heal others as they have been healed.

In the 2009 movie, *Avatar*, directed by James Cameron, we see the crippled war marine, Jake Sully, take over his dead brother's human/Na'vi hybrid—called an avatar—on the planet Pandora. The Na'vi, who are indigenous to Pandora, appear primitive but are highly evolved. As Jake integrates with the Na'vi, he falls in love with the people and the chief's daughter, Neytiri.

A human organization called the RDA attacks the Na'vi so they can mine the profitable mineral called unobtanium. Our hero, Jake, defeats the most terrifying predator on Pandora, which gains him ultimate Na'vi respect. He uses it to rally all the Na'vi tribes and animals to fight and defeat the RDA. After the battle, the remaining humans are sent away, and Jake finds his treasure, transferring the essence of his consciousness to his avatar and becoming a full Na'vi, to live the rest of his life on Pandora.

As I mentioned, this book is part of my Return phase. Coming to terms with my inner life and completing my hero's journey opened a whole new avenue of creativity for me. During my journey, I realized I wanted to pursue helping people again through education and mindful thinking, so I wrote this book and became a life coach. I am now living in my true authenticity and pursuing my purpose. Of course, my treasure is having attained a healthier ego, soul, and self, as well as pursuing my purpose, but it's my deepest wish that this book will serve as a story I brought back that helps you realize your own hero's journey.

As you have seen from my story, I was able to understand a great deal about my life by understanding what part of the hero's journey I was on at different times in my life. You may also consider using the hero's journey as a framework to gain insight into your own life. We may have numerous hero's journeys, each one an evolution in our growth. Some trips take a short time, some take longer. Each mini-journey within the lifelong journey brings us closer to mastering our worlds. Mini journeys happen over time. Your time away at college, raising your kids, the years in a past marriage, your first career. The events in our lives have a way of segmenting themselves when we take a bird's-eye view of them—unlike when we're living them. The hero's journey helps us reconcile the seeming randomness of our lives. By documenting our Preparation, Journey, and Return, we are granted insights to their purpose and why we needed to follow that path during that time. Looking back, we grasp the significance of life's lessons. Going forward, the hero's journey is a guiding metaphor for our future journeys.

Once you return home, you will take on the mentor role. It comes with the territory of having mastered your life. Your gifts and talents can now be generously passed onto others, especially to those that have just received the call. You will soon be the mentor helping shape other heroes on their journeys with what you have learned. Consider it a passing of the baton.

Knowing that all heroes (and all of us are heroes in our own stories) go through very hard times, but always move past them and are better off for it, is comforting. We can begin to see how our struggles strengthened us and how we are all heroes who can obtain the treasure life has to offer.

Keep in mind though, that heroes do the hard things and ask the tough questions that most people don't. Keep asking yourself if you are making a difference and contributing substance and significance.

RETURN PHASE

Stage Nine: The Reward

Identify a time in your life when you crossed the threshold, faced hardships (dragons) that you overcame, and claimed victory. Be aware though, that there will be at least one more challenge to face on your journey home with the reward.

Example:

In October of the year I was diagnosed, I was declared cancer free. I had conquered my fearful ordeal and won the battle with cancer. I was back on track, living my life, and consulting in Kansas.

Your Turn:

_____

_____

_____

Stage Ten: The Road Back

This is a critical stage because you must return home after the victory. Remember a time in your life where you had achieved victory and were on the road back home to the ordinary world. Again, you will still be tested further before reaching home.

Example:

At this stage in my life, the only chase scene I was experiencing was my dating failures. I was chasing my tail trying to find true love again. I was trying various ways to find my girlfriend, from meetups to online dating to hanging out in bars with no success stories.

Your Turn:

_____

_____

_____

Stage Eleven: The Resurrection

This may be the most interesting stage in the journey. It was for me, at least. Just when you think you have defeated your dragons and claimed victory on your way home, you are severely tested one more time. Think of a time in your life when after a victory you were tested or faced one more challenge that purified you with one last lesson. Remember that even though this challenge may be the most severe, you have been on your hero's journey and have gained valuable insights, skills, and mentors to help you face this last challenge.

Example:

I had been dating on and off since returning to Kansas, but nothing was even remotely serious until one day out of the blue I met a woman who would profoundly change the course of my life.

Your Turn:

_____

_____

_____

Stage Twelve: Return with the Treasure

You finally made it back to your ordinary world with treasure in hand. You have gained much insight and strength during your journey. Your reward is either something tangible, like a new job, a relationship, renewed health—or even more likely—an amazing story of survival to tell your tribe. Describe a time where you found your true, authentic self and were living your life purpose.

Example:

As I mentioned, this book is part of my Return phase. Completing my hero's journey opened a whole new avenue of creativity for me. During my journey I encountered many mentors and healers and through meditation and journaling I realized that I have always had a sense to help people through education.

Your Turn:

_____

_____

_____

EXERCISE 7
HAVE YOU FOUND YOURSELF?

These questions will help you decide if you have completed your journey or not.

- What is my personal kingdom, and what are my responsibilities to myself?

_____

_____

_____

- What are my responsibilities to other people?

_____

_____

_____

_____

_____

- Write a description of your role and responsibilities in the following areas of life:
- family
- primary relationship
- work
- church or community group

_____

_____

_____

_____

_____

- Is it your turn to give back and pay it forward? Are you prepared to be a mentor?

_____

_____

_____

_____

_____

_____

EXERCISE 8
HERO'S JOURNEY SUMMARY

Now that you have broken down your life according to the stages of the hero's journey it's time to put it all together and draw some conclusions. You want to figure out where in your life you have been the hero that was called to adventure, where you battled your metaphorical dragons and came out the victor. You also want to know where you refused the call. See if you can figure out why you refused the call for so long before you had the courage to cross the threshold and take your journey. What finally gave you the courage to move forward? Do you still have that courage today or have you lost it somehow?

Review all of your stages and put together a few paragraphs of what you have gleaned by sorting your life into stages of the hero's journey. If you get on a roll and find yourself writing pages and pages, by all means go for it. This can be a very cathartic and eye-opening experience. I know it was for me.

In later exercises you will be identifying your limiting stories, beliefs, and behaviors. You will want to use your hero's journey story to help identify those.

Example:

I started my adult life full of hope and passion. I wanted to live the American dream of owning a house in the suburbs, enjoying time with my wife, and watching my kids grow up. What I didn't realize is that I was predisposed to general anxiety disorder and as I pursued the dream I was piling on heaps of stress and secreting stress-producing hormones that were taking a toll on my body. Basically, I was in flight or fight all the time and the human body isn't made to function that way.

My hero's journey started when I heard the call to adventure in the shower one morning. But unfortunately, it would be more than nine years before I would accept the call and cross the threshold into the unknown world. My wakeup call was getting laid off and divorced in the span of one year. The Universe knocked me on my ass.

I struggled for years in the unknown world, drinking too much and feeling lonely, and then getting cancer. But I rallied and healed and made a comeback by helping others and writing about my experiences in life.

After I returned from my journey and claimed victory, I took up the mantle of mentor, wrote this book, and started life coaching to help people with life's challenges and to help them move forward as I did.

As this journey ends I embark on a new hero's journey, refining my purpose, building my business, and fostering new relationships.

Your Turn:

_____

_____

_____

_____

_____

_____

_____

_____

_____

SECTION TWO
TRANSFORMATION

CHAPTER 6
INSIDE-OUT THINKING

Now that we understand that we are the heroes of our own lives, you might be saying, okay, I get it, but I don't feel like a hero. As you saw from mythology and movies, heroes are made, not born. If you've identified parts of your life wherein you were a hero for moving through a difficult time and learning from it, that's amazing, right? But if you haven't identified yourself as a hero yet or know your hero skills could use some work, then there are proven ways to take that inner journey, find your bliss, supercharge your life, and become a superhero.

Creating lasting transformation takes new ways of thinking. The rest of this book is about transformation into your superhero self, but to do that it's going to be necessary to think differently. The next few chapters will present you with new ways to view your experience of life and what you think is reality.

The Human Experience

What makes up the human experience? Is it what we can feel, touch, and taste with our senses? The inside-out principles imply that mind, thought, and consciousness are the fundamental sources that make up the human experience. This inside-out concept had begun appearing in the literature under names ranging from "Psychology of Mind" to "Health Realization" to "The Three Principles of Mind, Consciousness, and Thought." The two most influential practitioners of this concept were Richard Carlson, author of *Don't Sweat the Small Stuff,* and Sydney Banks, a Scottish welder who had an enlightenment experience and was transformed from an uneducated worker in a pulp mill into a world-renowned guru and teacher.

The Mind

In the inside-out theory, the mind makes up the energy that runs through all things but in this case it's not the same as the brain, although mind energy is in our physical brains. It is what allows our hearts to beat, blood to flow, and mental activity to power our brains. The mind is not specific to you, it's the simple human energy and intelligence that runs through us all. As long as you are living, the mind is an engine that allows you to have the next heartbeat, the next breath, and the next thought—it literally turns on our experience of life.

Thought

We create our individual experience of reality via the vehicle of thought. Thought is the missing link between the formless world of pure potentiality and the created world of form. Without a thought, you can't have an experience. Without thought, we can't have a self or a notion of who we are. We create the understanding of ourselves via our thoughts. If you have an experience of something, it has to be in your thinking.

In Michael Neil's book, The Inside-Out Revolution, he points out that without thought, there would be no distinction between what is real and what is not. Thought is both the creator and substance of our beliefs and is the raw material of our ideas and dreams. We tend to be unaware of how much of life itself is created and maintained by thought. Much of what appears to be solid and real is actually part of the illusion of our thinking.

Consciousness

Consciousness is what brings our thinking to life and makes us aware of what we're thinking. It allows us to feel our thinking. It's kind of like the special effects department of the human system. Our thinking runs through our sensory system, giving us a super surround sound and high definition experience of our thoughts. If feels completely real and as if it's coming from something other than our thinking. But it's not. In order to feel anything, we have to be conscious. Consciousness is more powerful than the greatest Hollywood special effects team could ever be, because whatever we think, consciousness will bring to life in our body and make it feel absolutely real. The capacity to be aware and experience life is innate in human beings. It is a universal phenomenon. Our level of awareness in any given moment determines the quality of our experience.

The human mind can be viewed as an old-fashioned film projector. In thought, we create a picture of life and project it out on to the screen of our experience. We live in a movie of our own making.

THE MIND IS THE POWER SOURCE, THOUGHT IS THE FILM, AND CONSCIOUSNESS IS THE LIGHT SOURCE. ONE HUNDRED PERCENT OF OUR EXPERIENCE IS COMING FROM THE INSIDE OUT RATHER THAN THE OUTSIDE IN.

This concept clears up a lot of misconceptions and frustrations people have when they feel like the world is happening to them, as opposed to coming from within them. When you grasp this concept you essentially stop feeling at the mercy of things outside yourself. Thought is just temporary energy and basically not real. It comes into the mind and then goes. While it's there it can seem very real and compelling, but if you don't do anything with it, it will pass.

While most of us understand that thought is basically what we think about, we tend to be unaware of how much of life itself is created by thought. Much of what appears to be solid and real is actually part of the illusion of our thinking. Take icebergs for example. They appear solid but are actually made up of water. Just a small degree of fluctuation in temperature can destroy icebergs that have been around for hundreds of years. In our inner world, no matter how solid our reality may seem, it only takes a slight shift in consciousness for our entire world to change.

In this context, the phrase "this too shall pass" takes on a whole new meaning. If you give your mind the opportunity, it will self-correct and gravitate toward a clearer state of mind and an innate intelligence will come forth.

Thoughts can be seen as the media through which we experience life. Thoughts are actually energy that takes form in your head. When you are inside whatever form that thought takes, that's what you experience. It may be happy or sad, stressed, fearful, or even just what you want for dinner tonight. And here is a crucial point: When the volume is turned up on a thought or you hold it tightly, it has a larger effect on you. When you don't hold on tightly to your thinking or play it too loudly in your mind it just slides through, staying only briefly.

Generally, the louder and tighter our thinking gets, the more alone, frustrated, and frightened we become because we feel stuck.

That's why when something very traumatic happens in our lives it is harder to let go of it. The volume on that experience is turned way up. Yet when our thinking is quiet and more fluid we feel a sense of connection with people—our individual thoughts aren't so prominent and isolating, and we feel there is a flow moving life along on our behalf rather than having to make life happen.

Understanding this concept of inside-out thinking allows us to have insights into the nature of the human condition and opens up a higher perspective and a deeper understanding of what's really going on. The simple truth is this: Our experience of life is created from the inside out via the principles of mind, consciousness, and thought. We're living in the feeling of our thinking, not the feeling of the world.

Transformation

With an understanding of inside-out thinking then, how do we create true transformation and move into that comfortable feeling of trusting our innate wisdom?

The hero's journey lays out the perfect formula for creating a transformative shift in our lives. We are living in our normal, day-to-day existence when something happens in our lives that changes our point of view. This new view gives us the courage to make a change in our lives. We go from inaction to action, from stuck to flowing, from miserable to happy. We stop our numbing behaviors like smoking, drinking, or excessive shopping. Before long, our career takes off, relationships improve, and our creative output increases. Such a transformation is not the result of intervention, but rather the effect of a shift in our level of consciousness by understanding that we are and have been the heroes of our own lives. That we can handle what life dishes out to us because we have done it before and can do it again.

Remember the first time you fell in love? Suddenly the world seemed a more beautiful place. When in love, we are inspired to write poetry, draw pictures, or create things that reflect the beautiful feelings we felt inside. But because we attribute those feelings to another person, we often return to our old ways of thinking and feeling. Those feelings didn't come from outside of us, they are part of our essential selves. When we can see that fundamental truth, the shift in consciousness becomes permanent and a new way of seeing becomes available to us.

These transformative shifts are actually insights which are these wonderful "aha" moments when we're able to see something about ourselves, our lives, or life in general in a whole new way. If there is anything to be done, it comes effortlessly. In these wonderful transformative moments we find a fresh new way of seeing things that we may have been feeling for a long time. We just "get it," not intellectually the way we might understand a concept but at an almost cellular level. An insight is really just a new thought but can change our world, because you can have a fresh thought at any moment. Our thinking changes moment by moment, so the ability to have a new thought about an old situation is natural and ever present. Sometimes these thoughts seem to arise from somewhere beyond us and contain wisdom outside of our current knowledge. These are part of our natural intelligence of mind and we experience them as common sense, gut feelings, or innate wisdom.

Now that we have experienced a new insight we have a decision to make. We can continue to try and control life and attempt to think, behave, or change the world in our quest for happiness and well-being. This is where most people are; we'll find many companions on this path. Or we can take the path of transformation and give up our attachment to the comforting feelings of being in control. We give up the illusory safety of the known in search of the unknown—the field of all possibilities where miracles can happen.

When we can simply step into the realm of insight and be in the unknown, we can appreciate the mystery of being alive. While we don't control the timing of these perceptions, each time we have one we see life in a new and clearer way.

CHAPTER 7
QUANTUM CREATING — THOUGHTS BECOME THINGS

Have you heard the phrase, "thoughts become things?" Do you believe it? If you do, I bet you are constantly focusing all your attention on what you want instead of always thinking about your problems. Frankly, most of us focus way too much on our problems and how we can solve them. To create any real and lasting change in life, we need to find a way to overcome the years of our subconscious minds running the show. To do that, it will take a new way at looking at reality. You'll need to be open to some new interpretations of what is real and true. Stay with me—this is going to be fun.

Although the science of quantum physics and unified quantum field theory have been around for over a century and been written about by many credible scientists, the following accumulation of information that I'm about to share primarily comes from the esteemed Dr. Joe Dispenza. He has written many books on the concept of the quantum field and what he calls "quantum creating." We'll touch briefly on his theories and use them as a basis for creating lasting change and becoming true heroes in our lives.

To begin, let's start with a bit of history and science. What, not up for going back to grade school? I promise, this will be easy. In the seventeenth century, the scientific community, led by René Descartes and Isaac Newton, declared the physical world and the mind to be separate. Science focused on the material world and they left the mind up to God and religion, which lasted for many years. What they were saying was that humans have no influence on outcomes and that our reality was predetermined.

Quantum Physics to the Rescue

Then good old uncle Albert came along (that's Albert Einstein to you and me). His famous E=mc2 equation demonstrates that energy and matter are fundamentally related and that they are interchangeable. Thus the birth of quantum physics, which states that the most fundamental components or our world are both waves (energy) and particles (matter). The amazing thing is that determining which one is present depends solely on the observer. In essence, what we think is solid is actually in motion and is only solid when we observe it.

The old model showed the atom as mostly made up of a solid nucleus with smaller objects surrounding it. We now know that an atom is far from solid. In fact, it's 99.99999 percent energy and 0.00001 percent matter. So the atom is both energy and matter at the same time, but each state only exists momentarily. There is an infinite array of possibilities in an invisible field of energy, and only when we focus our attention on any one electron does it appear. In other words, a particle cannot show up until we observe it. Clearly, we can no longer view the mind and matter as separate.

What this means is that our mindful attention can effect change on matter and everything is pure potential. If one can use their mind to imagine something, because everything is a potential, then it already exists as a possibility in the quantum field. We just have to use our minds to bring that thought into reality.

Creating Change in Our Lives

With this new view of matter and the world, you can begin to see how we can affect lasting change in our lives. By increasing our skills of mindful focus of our thoughts and desires, we can create and live our chosen, authentic, and mission-driven lives and become the heroes we were meant to be.

But how can our thoughts and feelings create change? Dr. Dispenza explains that the quantum field can correlate to the Universe/God/Creator, as people use all these concepts when trying to understand how thoughts become things. He says the quantum field, or Universe/God/Creator, doesn't simply respond to vague wishes or thoughts. It only responds when the mind and body are aligned or coherent and are broadcasting the same signal. You must literally feel the feelings and emotions of the person you want to become in the moment, so you create a powerful electromagnetic frequency that broadcasts into the Universe/God/Creator (field of all possibilities). If we continue with our routine of known thoughts and feelings, we will just perpetuate the same old state, which created the same old behaviors, and will create the same old reality. Therefore, if we want to change our reality, we must think, feel, and act in new ways. We must be different in terms of our response to life's experiences. We need to generate a new electromagnetic signature that will match a potential reality in the Universe/God/Creator and have that potential reality pulled to us.

What You Say to Yourself Matters

You can see that what you say to yourself does matter and will determine your fate. You see, your subconscious mind pays attention to every thought and our only control is the type of instructions we provide it. If you think your life sucks, your subconscious hears that. You may not be aware that your negative self-talk is that big of a deal, but your subconscious takes it all in. It will attempt to give you what you want—it is very disciplined this way.

The problem is that your subconscious mind is not very good at deciphering moods, doubts, and fears. In fact, it cannot reason at all, as its only job is to obey your commands. Reasoning comes from your conscious mind only. When you tell yourself that today is going to be a bad day because that's just the way it's always been for you, your subconscious hears that and says, okay I heard you, and here is your bad day. Of course, you didn't mean for it to take what you said so literally, and you probably didn't realize you just commanded your subconscious to have a bad day. Our subconscious cannot distinguish our real intent. Everything we say passes to it without going through any filters.

For example, if you were joining a new school or a new job and you said to yourself, I probably won't bond with anyone here, so I might as well just sit here by myself in the lunch or break room, your subconscious mind will do everything in its power to grant the wish of not finding a friend. You were only saying that because you didn't want your feelings to be hurt if no one talked to you. But it is undermining your ultimate desire to be liked. The subconscious doesn't mean to do this of course; it's just following the orders you gave.

When something happens to us, we attach a meaning to it and hand it over to the subconscious for safe keeping. When a similar event in our life happens, it quickly provides us with a reaction to deal with the current situation based on this historical precedent. The problem is that these stories are sometimes very old and need updating.

Once we embrace that we are the culmination of every thought we've ever had, we can begin to recognize that we have created our world and we can take responsibility for it. It also allows us to know we have the power to change our world simply by changing our thoughts. We can rewrite our story through new thoughts and feelings.

For this to work though, you need to create a very coherent signal that you broadcast to the Universe/God/Creator. In physics, a coherent signal is made up of waves that are "in phase," which are powerful. The same goes for your thoughts and feelings. If you were an early follower of the law of attraction and were frustrated by not manifesting your dreams and wishes, it was probably due to the fact that thoughts alone don't create a coherent signal that is powerful enough. Creating a reality in the Universe/God/Creator only works when our thoughts and feelings are aligned.

To change our reality, we must also be surprised by the way these realities unfold. If you're trying to control the outcome, then you are playing the cause and effect game where you are waiting for something to happen in your outer experience before you validate it internally. So when you are manifesting your new reality, you want to hold a clear intention of what you want but leave the details to the unpredictable Universe/God/Creator.

Dr. Dispenza further suggests another quantum-manifesting rule that you should follow. You want to live in a state of gratitude as if you have already experienced your wanted reality. We are conditioned to believe that we need a reason to be grateful. We wait for an external reality to happen and then we are grateful that it appears in our lives. This is the old cause-and-effect model again. To truly be a quantum creator, we want to give thanks and feel the elevated emotions associated with a desired event before it occurs. We need to imagine this reality so completely that we begin to be in that future life in the present. We give thanks for something that exists as a potential in the Universe/God/Creator but has not yet happened in our reality. When we are in a state of gratitude, we transmit a signal into the field that an event has already occurred. This is more than an intellectual thought experiment. Your body, which only understands feelings, needs to feel as though you are living in your new reality right now.

Why Is It So Hard to Change?

Let's look at how the brain works. In *Breaking the Habit of Being Yourself*, Dr. Dispenza walks us through this complicated piece of grey matter called the brain so we can better understand why it's so hard to change, and also how, if we are consistent, we can begin to change who we are.

According to Dr. Dispenza, most people focus on three things in life: Their environment, their bodies, and time. To create a new you, though, you must think greater than the circumstances of your life and be greater than the feelings you have memorized in your body and live in a new line of time.

To effect change, you must have in your thoughts an idealized self (your hero model) that you can emulate, which is different from what exists today in your specific environment, body, and time.

One of the best examples of negative self-talk affecting attitude is exemplified by our favorite sad donkey, Eeyore, from the Winnie the Pooh stories. Even though we are amused by him, he is quite the negative self-talker. He says things such as, "It's not much of a tail, but I'm kind of attached to it," and "If it's a good morning, which I doubt... He says, "I'd say thistles, but nobody listens to me, anyway," and of course, "The sky has finally fallen. Always knew it would." Poor Eeyore has a bad case of thinking and saying thoughts that fulfill his sad outlook on life.

As we live our lives, our environment causes us to think, and familiar networks of nerve cells reflect previous experiences that are already wired in our brain. Essentially, we automatically think in familiar ways derived from memories. If our thoughts create our reality, and we keep thinking the same thoughts produced by the environment, then we will continue to create the same reality day after day. Our internal thoughts and feelings will match our external life, which is full of life's problems, conditions, and circumstances.

Now the outside environment is controlling our minds because we are repeatedly creating the same thoughts and reminding ourselves who we think we are based on our connection to the outer world. Our identity literally becomes defined by everything outside of us and we continually create the same old reality by thinking like we always have and creating more of the same old thing.

Stay with me here, I know it's getting deep. Basically, we wake up in the morning and follow the same routine, go to work, and do the same thing, then hurry home, do the same thing, and go to bed so we can do it all over the next day. The question is, why are we secretly expecting something different to show up in our life when we think the same thoughts, perform the same actions, and experience the same emotions every single day? After some time, our brains will create a finite set of circuits that create a very specific mental signature. We call this signature our personality. As long as our minds remain the same, our lives will stay the same.

Emotions = Chemicals = Addiction

Did you know that every time you have a thought there is a biochemical reaction in the brain? The chemical signal is released to the body as a message of thought. When the body gets these chemical messages from the brain, it complies by sending a matching set of reactions directly in alignment with what the brain is thinking. The body sends a confirming message back up to the brain that it's now feeling exactly the way the brain is thinking. We call this an emotion. Therefore, when you have happy and loving thoughts, you produce chemicals that make you feel the emotions of love and happiness. The same holds true if you have negative or fearful thoughts. In a matter of seconds, you begin to feel negative or fearful emotions. There is a moment-by-moment synchronicity between the brain and the body. Based on this chemical feedback loop, we think the way we feel and we feel the way we think. Therefore, we decide in the moment who we are based on our thinking and feeling and determine if we are angry or suffering or inspired or negative and so on. After years of thinking those same thoughts and feelings, we create a memorized state of mind and declare an "I am" statement. For example, I am angry, I am suffering, I am inspired. We are now defining ourselves as this state of mind and at this point, our thoughts and feelings have merged. We begin not only declaring our state of mind, but we start to say things like "I am a lazy person," or "I am a nervous person." We have created our personality state based on our thoughts and feelings.

Breaking a Habit

When we think about a highly charged past emotional experience, the brain fires in the exact sequence and pattern as before, solidifying the circuits into more hardwired networks. When the body can remember better than the conscious mind, the body becomes the mind. This is called a habit. We could also say that the body becomes the subconscious mind, which as I mentioned before, is a powerful 95 percent of the mind. Now we can begin to understand why it's so hard to change.

We may want to be happy, healthy, financially independent, and have wonderful relationships, but the experience of many years of suffering and the repeated cycle of chemicals being created have subconsciously conditioned the body to be in a habitual state of pain and suffering or at the very least in a stuck state. We are living in habit because we are no longer aware of what we are thinking, doing, or feeling—we are unconscious. We must break this habit of being who we have become.

This is exactly what happened to me when in my ordinary world. I was ignoring my mind and body and heaping piles of stress onto my system for years until my body just gave out. What followed were years of chronic pain that changed my brain. I was living every day in the habit of chronic pain and creating neural networks that when I moved a certain way or did anything strenuous, I would feel pain. Long after my emotional and physical scars healed, my brain still needed to unwire those chronic pain signals. I still have to work on reprogramming my old chronic pain brain daily into a healthy thinking and feeling brain.

Neural Networks

As I mentioned earlier in this book, neural networks are created in the brain. Before I became a life coach, I was an engineer in the telecommunications industry. I like to say that I single-handedly built the AOL network, which was basically a precursor to the internet. So, like Al Gore, I like to say that "I built the internet." All kidding aside, way back when I was engineering communication networks, we would install telephone switches (big computers) all over the world and would connect them with long distance telephone lines.

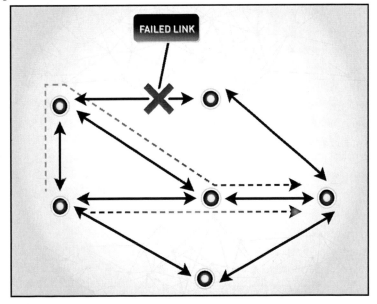

SIMPLE, WELL-DESIGNED TELEPHONE NETWORK. WHEN A SWITCH GOES DOWN, CALLS ARE TEMPORARILY REROUTED.

Our networks were designed so that if one switch went down, the calls would automatically be rerouted to other working switches to complete the calls. Usually, the downed switch would reboot and come back up quickly or we would send someone to fix it. Once the switch came back up, any new calls would be routed over the normal route using that repaired switch. This worked well and kept any one switch or network route from being overloaded.

But what would happen if, for some reason, that switch never came back up or got repaired? The calls would all be routed over that temporary backup route. The theory was that if a switch went down temporarily, the network would reroute traffic for a short time without any detrimental effects or dropped calls. But if all the traffic were to be rerouted over the backup route for a long time, it would not function properly because the network wasn't engineered that way. It would, in effect, become a hard-wired path

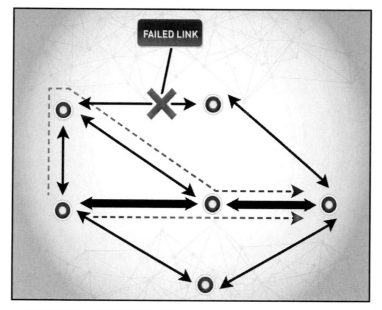

A DISTORTED NETWORK WITH AN ABNORMALLY LARGE AND INEFFICIENT CIRCUIT.

for calls but wouldn't be as efficient or helpful to the network. Soon the network would automatically route calls over this inefficient circuit.

Eventually, though, what would happen is that we would just add more switches to the backup route and create a larger and more robust network based on this new route because it was sometimes easier to add a switch to the backup route then to fix the broken switch that caused the reroute in the first place. So now our network looked different and there were very large phone circuits in an area that didn't need them there.

We had this distorted-looking network with very large circuits or bandwidth in certain areas that didn't make sense. They worked well and tons of calls flowed over them, but it was costing us more money because it wasn't the most efficient use of our resources. We had let the outside environment dictate how our network worked.

What I have just described is what happens in our brains when we let the outside world dictate how we think, feel, and act. Dr. Dispenza likes to refer to the phrase "nerve cells that fire together, wire together." The official name for this behavior theory is called Hebb's Law. It states that if you repeatedly activate the same nerve cells, then each time they turn on, it will be easier for them to fire in unison again and eventually, those neurons will develop a long-term relationship. So just like my communication networks, when I say thoughts, behaviors, or feelings are hardwired, I mean that clusters of neurons have fired together many times in the very same way and have organized themselves into specific patterns and connections. The more these networks of neurons fire, the more they wire into static routes of activity. Eventually, whatever the thoughts, behaviors, or feelings included in those neural networks are, they will become an automatic subconscious habit. Just like the backup circuits of a communication network can reroute calls, our brains can reroute neurons to create neural networks based on either the way it was designed to efficiently run or based on the outside world. What I am saying is that, of course, you don't want to create neural networks based on the unpredictable and often negative outside world with all its potential problems, but rather, you want to create your own positive highly efficient and smooth-running neural networks.

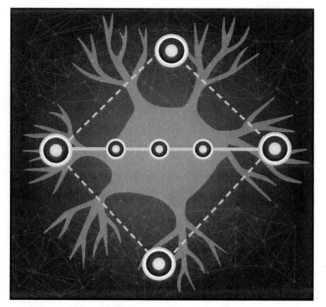

NEURAL NETWORK IN THE BRAIN.

The good news is that since we created these crazy, misguided, and negative neural network loops, we can uncreate them and put an end to letting the outside environment control our minds and lives. To do so though, we must fundamentally change the way we think, act, and feel. Because the way we think, feel, and act is called our personality and it's what creates our personal reality. Am I saying that to become our own heroes and live a purpose-driven life we must create a new personality? Absolutely! That's exactly what I'm saying. The good news is there are practical ways and steps to do it and I'll be here to guide you through it all.

Change Your Thoughts, Change Your Life

Neuroscience has proven that we can change our brains—and therefore our behaviors, attitudes, and beliefs—just by thinking differently (in other words, without changing anything in our environment). Through mental rehearsal (repeatedly imagining performing an action), the circuits in the brain can reorganize themselves to reflect our objectives. We can make our thoughts so real that the brain changes to look like the event has already become a physical reality. Our thoughts can become our experience.

Athletes and sports psychologist have known this for years. Most high performing athletes visualize their performance in their minds prior to actually performing them on the court, field, or course. They visualize every last detail of every swing, shot, catch, or throw done in perfect rhythm and form. As they do this their minds can't tell the difference than if they were actually performing those moves in the outside world. If high performing athletes can do this, so can we to create our mission and purposeful life.

Most of us live in the past and resist living in a new future because our bodies are so used to memorizing the chemical records of our past experiences that they grow attached to these emotions. We become addicted to those familiar feelings. When we are in the midst of an experience, our brain receives information from the external environment through the senses (sight, smell, sound, taste, and touch). As that cumulative sensory data reaches the brain and is processed, networks of neurons arrange themselves into specific patterns, reflecting the external event, while the brain releases emotional chemicals. The more intense the experience, the more emotional chemicals will flood the body and the more we will pay attention to whoever or whatever was in our external environment that caused the change. That event is now called a memory, and it includes the feelings and emotional chemical signatures of that event. Feelings and emotions are a chemical record of past experiences.

The only way we can change ourselves is to think beyond our past and how we feel. Accomplishing this feat is the great challenge of personal change. Thoughts and emotions are not bad, they are just the end products of experience. But if we are always reliving the past, we can't embrace new experiences.

The Dreamers

Think of any number of great historical figures like Abraham Lincoln, Martin Luther King, Nelson Mandela, or even Michael Jackson and Michael Jordan. Do you know what they all had in common aside from greatness? They all had a dream or vision that was deep within them and was so present in their existence that they lived and breathed their destiny. They vividly saw in their minds what they would become or achieve or create ahead of it ever having happened. In other words, they behaved as if what they saw for their life was already a reality. They had no doubt that their vision would be real during their lives. When our thoughts and feelings are coherent, when our minds and our bodies work together, when our words, deeds, and actions are aligned, there is nothing that can't happen. Quantum physics demands it.

My client, R.A., created a limiting belief when she was young that no one ever chose her for anything and felt left out. As an adult this manifested in her as low self-esteem. Even though she created a nice life for herself as a mother, wife, and business owner, she felt like she could have and do and be more. Once we identified this limiting belief of no one chooses her, she began to see how she constantly reminded herself that she isn't one who deserves to be chosen and she learned to accept mediocrity in her life and business. When she started her business her negative thoughts and emotions kept her from being as successful as she could be. After we worked to realize that her limiting belief was not true, she began to change her self-talk, her emotions around self-worth got better, and her business started to take off.

Changing Our Genetics

Before we dive into the specifics of how we go about creating lasting change, let me talk about one more amazing area that was once believed to be static, like our brains. I'm talking about our physical health and our genes. Most people think we must live with the genes we were dealt with. This may be true of the DNA strands that we inherit, but the science of epigenetics shows us that genes can change or the gene function can change without a change in the DNA. We now know that the environment, by activating or deactivating particular genes, has the most effect on our health. According to Dr. Dispenza, less than 5 percent of all diseases today stem from single gene disorders. Whereas 95 percent of all illnesses are related to lifestyle choices, chronic stress, and toxic factors in the environment. This is amazing news because it shows that we have much more control over our health than was once believed. By changing our internal state of mind, we overcome the effects of a stressful or toxic environment so that certain genes do not become activated. We may not be able to control all the conditions in our external environment, but we certainly have a choice in controlling our inner environment.

We now know that genes are as changeable as our brains. Just by changing our thoughts, feelings, and emotions and making healthier lifestyle choices regarding nutrition and stress, we send our cells new signals, which can express new functions without changing the genetic code. Just like we can change who we have been, we can signal our genes to create beneficial health.

Living in Survival Mode—The Stress Response

By now, we've all heard of the stress response and how we were created with the ability to turn on what's called the "fight or flight" response. This is our ancient survival mechanism that is doing its job. If there is a tiger in a bush and you are walking by, you better believe there is a tiger in there. If you just whistle on by thinking positive thoughts, "there's not tiger here, I'm not afraid of tigers," you may end up tiger food. If, on the other hand, you sense there is a tiger in the bushes and react appropriately, your thinking just saved you by first alerting your brain and body that it better get ready to run or fight something to stay alive.

However, we are the only animal that can turn on the fight or flight response by thought alone, even if that thought has nothing to do with our present reality or not. We can turn on that stress response in anticipation of the future. But even more devastating is the fact that we can produce the same stress response by thinking about an unhappy memory. Our bodies are either existing in the future or the past. No organism was designed to deal with the negative effects of stress when it is constantly turned on. When we can't turn off the stress response, we are headed for a breakdown in the body. Been there, done that, and it's not fun.

The overproduction of stress hormones creates emotions of anger, fear, envy, and hatred, which can create feelings of aggression, frustration, anxiety, and insecurity and cause us to experience pain, suffering, sadness, hopelessness, and depression. The stress response forces us to focus on and obsess about the body, the environment, and time. Thus, we begin to define our "self" within the confines of the physical realm; we become less spiritual, less conscious, less aware, and less mindful. Living in survival mode causes us to focus on the 0.00001 percent instead of the 99.99999 percent of reality.

Living in Creation to Forget Ourselves

The alternative to living in survival mode is to live in creation mode. When we are in the midst of creating, we forget about ourselves.

When one dissociates from the known world and is no longer

someone who associates identity with things one owns, or people one knows, or tasks one does, or places one has visited, one becomes selfless, moving beyond time and space to pure awareness. Once one is no longer connected to a body and no longer focused on people, places, or things in the external environment, one can enter the quantum field.

We all have the ability to observe our own thoughts and selves. We can decide that we no longer want to be and act, think, or feel the same way we always have. This ability to self-reflect allows us to modify our behaviors so we can achieve something newer, better, and greater.

Remember, energy flows where attention goes. To use our attention to empower our new life, we must first figure out what we have already created in the old us. We need to look at our limiting beliefs about life, ourselves, and others which we will cover extensively in the next chapter. Our lives are dictated by our beliefs. Our beliefs are the thoughts we keep consciously or unconsciously, accepting them as the law in our lives. Whether we are aware of them or not, they still affect our reality. We must go in deep and look at things we probably have been unaware of before. We must unearth our subconscious thoughts, reflexive behaviors, and automatic emotional reactions, and put them under a microscope and determine if they are true or not. Most likely, a lot of our limiting beliefs were created when we were very young, up to six years of age, and they are most likely not true.

The purpose of becoming self-aware is so that we will no longer allow any thoughts, actions, or emotions we don't want to experience to pass by our awareness. We want to consciously inhibit any of these limiting beliefs so we don't continue firing and wiring the old neural networks. We can begin to prune away the old neural hardware. The goal here is to unlearn the old personality so we can free up space for the new personality and the new future that we will be creating.

One of the ways we are going to create our new personality is to set aside time to think about a new way of thinking and feeling. We can imagine fresh new possibilities by asking ourselves important questions about what we want, who we want to be, and what we want to change in our lives. Once we have figured out what we want to be, we can begin to mentally rehearse these new ways of thinking and feeling. By continually practicing these thinking and feeling sessions, we will start rewiring ourselves neurologically to a new mind. The more we can "re-mind" ourselves, the more we'll change our brains and our lives.

Meditate to Change

Let's look at how we can circumvent our natural tendencies to create thoughts and feelings from external experiences. This process is backed by real science and is not a "fake it until you make it" trick. We can create a new reality by creating a new way of thinking and being. If you have ever thought of something that hasn't happened yet, like what you're going to have for dinner this evening or the speech you need to give tomorrow at work, you can create your new reality. Your thinking about those future events was to the exclusion of everything else that was happening to you at that very moment. Your body started to move into that being just by your thinking it alone. You probably started to feel hungry after thinking about your dinner, or your body may have tensed up as you thought about the speech you had to give. Your mind and body started to be one. Can you use this same concept to create the reality you want and become your own hero? You absolutely can, and you can do it via the meditation and visualization process I am going to show you. Meditation allows us to change our brains, bodies, and our state of mind. We can make these changes from the comfort of our couch or chair with no external experience whatsoever. Through meditation and visualization, we can install new, hardwired neural networks.

The meditative process allows you to create a new state of mind and being by bringing together all the information learned and wired synaptically into your brain about what it means to be the kind of person you want to become. For example, if you wanted the new you to be a fierce competitor, all you must do is think about being a fierce, intense winner. You already know what being a fierce competitor is from watching sports or movies or participating in sports, and you know what it looks and feels like. Now you get to pick and choose from the knowledge and experience to create the new ideal of yourself.

Once you have created those thoughts and feelings in your mind, you have activated new circuits in new ways to create a holographic image that gives you a model to follow in creating your future reality. You simply must use your knowledge and experience of the feeling or emotion you want to create, to create an emotional state in your meditation/visualization.

How will you know that your meditation/visualizations are working? You will feel differently and act differently, and signs from the Universe/God/Creator will visit you in unexpected ways. If you feel the same as you did before, then nothing has happened in the Universal field. Your same thoughts and feeling are reproducing the same electromagnetic signal to the field. You must stay committed and not get up from your meditation/visualization session until you are that new person with new thoughts, feelings, and emotions that you have selected in advance. You are now the designer of your life. Your job is to live into your new reality by continually doing your meditation/visualization. You're changing the inside of you, which will eventually change the outside of you. You have broken that old Newtonian concept of something external controlling your thoughts, actions, and emotions.

If you have tried to live by the law of attraction before but never achieved the life you wanted, it's possible that you've been living by a negative memorized emotion that has become so much a part of your identity on a subconscious level that you cannot feel any other way. Doing the exercises and meditation/visualizations that I am about to show you will finally break you free of these limiting and life-crippling beliefs once and for all.

CHAPTER 8
THE TRANSFORMATIONAL LADDER —
FIND YOUR BLISS

Joseph Campbell tells us that true heroes find their bliss and give their gifts to the world. That's the ultimate treasure claimed from the courageous hero's journey. Now that you understand how a healthy person progresses psychologically through life, know that you can be the hero of your life, and believe it's possible to create this new hero, it's time to find your bliss and complete your hero's journey. The following exercises will help peel back the layers of what I call the "transformational ladder" and create your new self using empowering thoughts and beliefs.

You can either fill in the answers here in this chapter or print out the appendix, which has all the exercises in one place.

No matter if you are stuck in the middle of your hero's journey or have completed many hero's journeys, there is always room for improvement. Human suffering comes from the illusion that we are not enough. This is universal for humans and it starts in young childhood when we are completely at the mercy of our parents to support us in life.

The transformational ladder will guide you from defining your limiting behaviors down through the limiting stories you tell yourself and what emotions are causing the main limiting beliefs that were created by original life-triggering events. With this information, you will be ready to move on to climbing back up the ladder with new empowering beliefs, emotions, stories, and behaviors and become the hero of your life.

The exercises below will help you figure out where you are stuck in life and will give you insight on how to get unstuck and move forward in your journey. If you have completed the exercises in Section One on the hero's journey, you can already see how your life has unfolded into your journey. Now it's time to go deep and define what you want to change in your life and why. It's your job to look back on your life and figure out where things may have gone wrong or where unfortunate circumstances took place and what meaning you attached to those life events. As you use the exercises to uncover your personal growth pattern, you will begin to see yourself as the hero of your own life and how your life has shaped your journey so far. With this knowledge, you will peel back the onion of your transformational ladder and sit with this knowledge for a while. With a clear understanding of how your past life might have contributed to your limiting beliefs and actions, you will rebuild your ideal hero life.

Uncovering Where You Are Stuck

The first step to change is admitting you are stuck. Where are you stuck in your life? These are areas where you are most frustrated, annoyed, disappointed, feeling helpless. The primary feelings of being stuck are powerlessness, hiding, and frustration. Some examples might be:

- You are stuck in a relationship you know isn't working.

- You are stuck in a job that is sucking the life out of you.

- You have lost your connection to your faith.

- You never have enough money.

- You are overweight.

- You are out of shape.

- Your family doesn't support you.
- You have chronic pain.

List where you feel you are stuck:

1. _____

2. _____

3. _____

4. _____

5. _____

Now take a few minutes to reflect on these stuck areas of your life above by answering the following questions.

How have you ignored these stuck areas or used them as excuses?

_____

_____

_____

How long have these stuck areas been with you? Are you repeating a pattern?

_____

_____

_____

Can you remember the first time you felt stuck in these areas?

_____

_____

_____

Do you believe that staying stuck in these areas benefited you in any way?

_____

_____

_____

Do you have any relationships in your life that support you being stuck in these areas?

_____

_____

_____

Why Must You Change?

Let's get clear on why you must change. What have you missed out on because you let fear and apathy rule your life? List your missed opportunities below.

- **Romance:**
  - _____

- **Career:**
  - _____

- **Health:**
  - _____

- **Spirituality:**
  - _____

- **Relationships:**
  - _____

- **Finances:**

  - _____

- **Volunteering:**

  - _____

- **Add Your Own Category** _____:

  - _____

Make a list of all the things you want in your life. What do you want to feel? What do you want to do with your life? What things do you want to have in your life? Whom do you want to love?

1. _____
2. _____
3. _____
4. _____
5. _____

Write out why you must commit to changing now (be as detailed as possible).

_____

_____

_____

_____

- **What is the worst that could happen if you don't change now?**

  - _____

  - _____

- **What's the worst thing that could happen if you decide to change now?**

  - _____

  - _____

- **Has the Universe/God/Creator tried to get your attention recently? What were the signs?**

  - _____

  - _____

Now that you have identified where you are stuck, why you must change, and what you want out of life, you will dive into your emotions and what limiting beliefs, stories, and events have held you back.

What differentiates between a belief, an emotion, a story, and a behavior in this context? When you have an early trauma or crisis in your life, a belief is the meaning that you created from that traumatic event. Beliefs create emotions or a felt sense in the body. Your emotions create your stories or how you describe your circumstances. Your stories create your behaviors or how you repeatedly react to your circumstances.

We are wired to assign meaning to what happens to us in life. The amazing thing, though, is that no one else can assign meaning to our life events. Only we can do that. That should make you feel very hopeful.

Your Limiting Stories, Beliefs, Emotions, Thinking, and Behaviors

Our behaviors are usually driven by the stories we tell ourselves. We don't just do things randomly. Our thoughts create our behavior. Every behavior was first a thought or story.

Identifying Your Limiting Stories

- There are all kinds of stories that hold you back. Common ones are:
- The world is not a safe place.
- I'm too old.
- I'm too fat.
- I don't have enough time.
- I don't have enough money.
- I'm too young.
- Life will never get better.
- This is all I'm worth.
- I've always been this way.
- I don't feel I can be my true self.
- My children's happiness is more important than my own.
- My parents don't approve of who I am.
- Life doesn't support me.
- I'm cursed.
- This works for other people but not for me.

What stories are you telling yourself? Write them down.

1. _____

2. _____

3. _____

4. _____

5. _____

Where Did Your Limiting Stories Come From?

As you ask yourself where your limiting stories come from, remember not to beat yourself up. Be kind and gentle with yourself as you look at the hard parts of your life and trust the process. Go back and read what you wrote about the stories you tell yourself. Allow yourself to soak them in. Don't push them away. Then ask yourself, did I hear these stories from someone else first? Consider these influential sources:

- parents
- significant others
- religious leaders
- bosses
- brothers or sisters
- the media
- bullies in school
- friends
- extended family members
- role models

Try and think about the actual words that these people said to you. Common examples are:

- Finish what's on your plate; there are starving kids in India.
- You'll never amount to anything.
- You're going to be just like your mother/father.
- Children should be seen and not heard.
- No one in this family has ever gone to college. What

makes you think you can?

- Don't air your dirty laundry in public.

List the top five times when you first heard these limiting stories and what they were.

1. _____

2. _____

3. _____

4. _____

5. _____

Identifying Your Limiting Beliefs

Beliefs are in many ways the origin of the stories we tell about life. Beliefs are more powerful than stories because beliefs are based on the meaning we gave past events in our lives. In other words, belief determines how we see or perceive events. Like a filter. And a story is the account of what happened or what will happen based on your beliefs. Some examples are:

- I'll never get a new job.

- No one ever listens to me.

- He always makes me feel angry.

- Everyone uses me.

- I want to call it quits.

- Today is a bad day for me, so why bother trying to change it.

- It's her fault that my life is this way.

- I'm really not that smart.

- I honestly can't change. Maybe it would be better to start another time.

- I don't feel like it.

- My life sucks.

- I hate my situation with _____.

- I'll never make a difference. I can't.

- _____ does not like me.

- I have to work harder than most people.

- It's my genetics. I am just like my mother/father.

Review the stories you tell yourself and where they came from and turn them into belief statements. List your limiting beliefs here:

1. _____

2. _____

3. _____

4. _____

5. _____

Identifying Your Limiting Emotions

Go back to the list you created of the limiting thinking, stories, and beliefs that hold you back. Reread them. Then bring your awareness to your body. How are you feeling as you read these stories, thoughts, and beliefs, and where are you feeling it? Some people feel these deep strong emotions in their stomachs or jaws. Others feel them manifest as weakness in their legs. Pay attention to where you feel them.

Right now we are just going to sit with those feelings rather than acting on them. If this brings up panic, fear, and shame, that is okay. There is nothing wrong with you. Remember, you are not your feelings and emotions.

I usually feel my deep emotions in my throat and solar plexus. Where do you feel your deep emotions?

Think of all the times your limiting stories, thoughts, and beliefs have held you back. Look at the pain you've caused others. Look at the pain you've caused yourself. Look how you have kept yourself small, how you've put others first and denied your own worth and intuition. Look back over your hero's journey life and see how you've held yourself back. Notice how this makes you feel and where you feel it in your body.

Naming Your Emotions

Now that you have gotten in touch with your emotions, list five emotions that you feel as a result of these limiting behaviors and stories and the areas in your body where you feel them.

If it is hard to access your emotions, or if you're getting frustrated that you aren't feeling anything, this is good. You're feeling frustrated. Where do you feel that in your body? Just because you don't feel the emotions you think you should be feeling doesn't mean you can't feel. Your job is to go with whatever is present in the here and now. Some common emotions are:

- anger
- hate
- powerlessness
- guilt
- shame
- sadness

- unworthiness

- betrayal

- regret

- depression

- stress

- self-doubt

- lack of belonging

- resentment

List your emotions and where you feel them in your body.

I feel _____ in my _____.

I feel _____ in my _____.

I feel _____ in my _____.

I feel _____ in my _____.

I feel _____ in my _____.

These are difficult things to feel, and you may want to turn back, but don't. Stay with them. These feelings will pass and fade away. These emotions do not control you. In fact, feeling them is the first step toward setting yourself free.

Identify Your Limiting Thinking

Next ask yourself: How do I think when I feel this way? For example, if you want to get rid of the feeling of shame, ask yourself: What is my attitude when I feel shame? You might say you are scared or timid or quiet and shy. An attitude is a series of thoughts connected to a feeling. You need to define the habit that has been created by these emotions. You may develop attitudes that are:

- competitive
- blaming
- desperate
- overly intellectual
- lazy
- dishonest
- controlling
- needy
- sensitive
- insensitive

List your own top five attitudes.

1. _____

2. _____

3. _____

4. _____

5. _____

Most of your actions, behaviors, and choices have made you act in predictable ways. Right now, consider these emotional attitudes without doing anything. Just observe them.

Identifying Your Limiting Behaviors

Your stories create your behaviors or how you repeatedly react to your circumstances. What behaviors do you blame yourself for doing and yet can't seem to find a way past?

Some of these behaviors might be:

- self-sabotage
- overeating
- blaming others
- withdrawing or hiding
- lying
- abusing porn
- abusing gambling
- cheating on your partner

List your limiting behaviors here:

1. _____
2. _____
3. _____
4. _____
5. _____

Uncovering Your Triggering Life Events

We are going to go back to a time of hurt—a time you have pushed away for so long, a time that you may even have pretended didn't happen and that you don't want to talk about. It is your moment or moments of trauma, pain, and original hurt.

These triggering life events are moments in our past when something happened and we decided to form beliefs about the world. They come from all kinds of places. They can be something as simple as being left behind at school, a kid calling you fat, or the tone in which a parent said something to you as a child. Or they could be more extreme, like sexual, emotional, or physical abuse.

The majority of these triggering life events start before the age of 10. Because they are never addressed or worked through, these limiting beliefs carry themselves into adulthood. In order to change your story these triggering life events must be seen with new eyes. It's time to uncover how you created these limiting beliefs to protect yourself long ago. It may take running through this process a few times to find all the triggering life events. Common triggering life events include:

- sexual abuse
- physical abuse
- emotional abuse
- violent family members
- being required to be perfect, rather than yourself
- being abandoned by one or both parents
- a parent's addiction
- needing to be the caregiver of your parent as a child
- other people condemning you
- being made fun of at school
- witnessing violence
- the death of a loved one
- not being recognized by your father
- not being nurtured by your mother

Go back and read your top five limiting beliefs. Take a minute to let the emotions to wash over you.

Now list the triggering life events that shaped your beliefs.

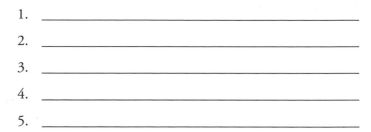

1. _____

2. _____

3. _____

4. _____

5. _____

Admitting Who You Are

Acknowledge your true self rather than the self you show to other people. Allow yourself to be vulnerable. Tell the Universe/God/Creator who you have been and what you want to change about yourself and admit what you are hiding.

Owning up to who we really are, what our past mistakes have been, and asking to be accepted are among the most challenging things for us to do as humans. This works because we are admitting our faults and failures to our higher power and not to another similarly flawed human.

Close your eyes and become still and begin to tell this higher power who you have been. Share the details of the stories that you have carried around with you. Some examples might be:

- I am afraid of falling in love because it hurts too much.

- I pretend I am happy, but I am really suffering because I am lonely.

- I do not want anyone to know that I feel so guilty, so I lie about myself.

- I lie to people so that they like me and so I won't feel unloved and unworthy.

- I can't stop feeling self-pity. I think, act, and feel this way all day long because I do not know how else I can feel.

- I have felt like a failure most of my life, so I try extra to be a success.

Write down what comes up for you.

_____

_____

_____

_____

_____

Creating the New You—Climbing Back up the Transformational Ladder

Up until now you've worked at identifying your limited thinking and pruning away old synaptic connections. Now it's time to sprout new ones so that the new mind you create will become the platform for who you will be in your future. Let's find your bliss and create a new you. Your daily meditations, contemplations, and rehearsals will be like tending to a garden to yield a great expression of the new you. You should fall in love with the vision of who you are becoming. Love is a higher frequency emotion than those in survival emotions that allowed the negative and limiting beliefs to control your subconscious thinking.

In the 2006 movie, *The Pursuit of Happyness,* directed by Gabriele Muccino, Will Smith stars as Chris Gardner, a person who has everything go wrong in his life. The film shows that even someone with these misfortunes can succeed by never giving up. Chris Gardner continues to tell himself and everyone around him that he will succeed and be able to provide for his son. My favorite scene from the movie is when Chris is talking to his son on the basketball court.

"Don't ever let someone tell you that you can't do something," he says. "Not even me. You got a dream? You got to protect it. People can't do something themselves they want to tell you, you can't do it. You want something, go get it. Period."

Focus on the positive, redirect your negative self-talk to positive, and never give up. This is how heroes live and return with the treasure of a purpose-driven and fulfilling life.

Below are a series of open-ended questions that will cause you to think in different ways than you normally think and to entertain new possibilities. This turns on your frontal lobe. You are creating the platform of the new self by forcing the brain to fire in novel ways.

Write down answers to as many questions as seem relevant to you. After you complete the answers, review, reflect, analyze and think about all the possibilities your answers raise. You will then be climbing the transformational ladder with new beliefs, emotions, stories, and behaviors.

How Do I Want to Think?

- What is my ideal self?

  - _____

  - _____

- What historical figures do I admire?

  - _____

  - _____

- After whom do I want to model my own behavior? How would I be if I were like them?

  - _____

  - _____

- What would I say to myself if I were this new person I want to be?

  - _____

  - _____

How Do I Want to Act?

- How would the "new me" act?

  - _____

  - _____

- What would I do? How do I see myself behaving?
  - _____
  - _____

- How would I talk to others if I were changed?
  - _____
  - _____

- What would my new attitude be?
  - _____
  - _____

- What do I want to believe about the new me?
  - _____
  - _____

- How do I want to be perceived?
  - _____
  - _____

- What would I say to myself if I were this person?
  - _____
  - _____

- How would this person act?
  - _____
  - _____

- How Do I Want to Feel?

    - _____

    - _____

- What would I feel if I were my ideal self?

    - _____

    - _____

- What would my energy be like as this new ideal?

    - _____

    - _____

Now that you have brainstormed how you want to think, feel, and act differently, it's time to get specific on your new empowering stories, beliefs, thinking, and behaviors. Review your limiting stories, beliefs, thinking, and behaviors and rewrite them into positives statements.

What Are the Stories That Will Move You Forward?

List five new, empowering stories that will move you forward.

1. _____

2. _____

3. _____

4. _____

5. _____

What Are the Beliefs That Will Move You Forward?

1. _____

2. _____

3. _____

4. _____

5. _____

List five new, empowering beliefs that will move you forward.

1. _____

2. _____

3. _____

4. _____

5. _____

What New, Empowering Thinking Will Move You Forward?

1. _____

2. _____

3. _____

4. _____

5. _____

List five new, empowering thoughts that will move you forward.

1. _____

2. _____

3. _____

4. _____

5. _____

What Behaviors Will Move You Forward?

1. _____

2. _____

3. _____

4. _____

5. _____

List five new, empowering stories that will move you forward.

1. _____

2. _____

3. _____

4. _____

5. _____

Your Hero Life Moment

Step 1: What Is Your Hero Moment?

Imagine a time in your life when you accomplished or did something that made you feel absolutely incredible. A time where you felt empowered, confident, happy, and full of energy. A time in your life when you felt like you could do anything you put your mind to. It can be *any* time in your life. When you were a kid hitting a home run, acing a test, leaving your job, getting a big check, accomplishing something significant, falling in love, speaking on stage, or doing something you had never done before and crushing it.

_____

_____

_____

Step 2: What Was the Most Powerful Part of Your Hero Life Moment?

_____

_____

_____

Redefine the idea. Pinpoint it all the way down to one specific moment. For examples, pride upon receiving an award, the feeling of crossing home plate after the game-winning home run, the sound of the crowd during a standing ovation, the feeling of looking at an "A" on your final exam.

Step 3: Why Is that Moment so Significant for You?

_____

_____

_____

Attach meaning to it. What does it mean to you? For example, perhaps you accomplished something great before and now you know you can do it again. Or you stepped outside your comfort zone and believe you can do it again. You can do anything if you put your mind to it.

_____

_____

_____

Step 4: Physiologically, How Did You Feel During Your Hero Moment?

What did you feel, how did you stand, how were you breathing, what did you hear?

_____

_____

_____

If you can have that happen to you back then, what is holding you back now? What if you could achieve something this amazing now?

What if you thought about this moment every day and recreated that physiological response in your body? You can leverage this for any project, event, or anytime you want to get pumped up empowered to take action.

Discovering Your Purpose and Passion

Passion and purpose are similar but distinct. They are connected and seductive to us all.

The following exercises will help draw out the purpose and passion that resides within you. Don't come at this with preconceived ideas of what your purpose is or should be or what others think it should be.

Take your time with these questions. The answers you seek will be revealed when you go inward with calmness, patience, and vulnerability.

Think about what makes you tear up.

- When you are emotionally moved, it is a sign of what resonates within you, either good or bad, happy or sad. We all have something that triggers our emotions and feelings. Describe what that is for you.

_____

_____

What makes you angry and annoyed?

- What kinds of things make you really mad and sometimes push you over the top?

- When you declare what makes you angry you are leaving clues as to what you are passionate about.

_____

_____

_____

What charges and recharges you?

- What inspires and motivates you?

- Is it nature? Is it when you are being creative? Do you like working in groups or by yourself? Does music inspire you? What kind?

- The answers to this question are closely connected to your purpose and passion.

_____

_____

_____

What are you better at than anyone else you know?

- This is when you are in your flow zone and quite often lose track of them when you're doing this.

_____

_____

_____

What can people count on you to always do?

- This is where you walk your talk and find it easy to do.

- People have been telling you this your whole life.

- At work, what are you the go-to person for?

- In your family, what is it that you always do?

_____

_____

_____

When will you be worthy?

- What needs to happen for you to feel truly worthwhile? Remember we are hardest on ourselves.

_____

_____

_____

- How will you know when you have "arrived?" When will your credibility be irrefutable?

_____

_____

_____

What gift will you share with the world?

- Your gift may be connected to your deepest desires.

_____

_____

_____

Who or what would you die for?

- What means the most to you? Who would you make the

ultimate sacrifice for?

- When you know what you would die for it grants you the wisdom of knowing what to live for.

- Think about what's in it for you.

When your time is up what would your final wish be?

- How will you use it?

- What will it be for?

- Who will benefit?

- When all you have is one wish left, your answer will be very revealing. Your purpose and passion are rooted in your values. You're not allowed to ask for more time.

How do you want to be remembered?

- When you think about this, what would honor your memory the most?

- What stories would you most like to hear told about you at your funeral?

- The answers to this question are what are most important to you. These are the traits and attributes you value the most in life.

- This is how you want to live your life.

_____

_____

_____

Your passion and purpose are in the answers above. You are the hero of your own life.

Creating the New You

You've unpacked your limiting thinking, figured out your why, and created new, empowering thinking as you climbed back up the transformational ladder. You have figured out your mission and what you're passionate about. Now it's time to take these new, empowering views, follow your bliss, and create the hero of your life. This part of the exercise will include creating powerful daily personal meditations and visualizations.

- Hold the image of you being or doing the things that you want this new you to be or do. You are the quantum creator, commanding matter to conform to your intentions.

- With clarity, hold the image of each manifestation in your mind for a few seconds, and then let it go into the quantum field to be executed by the Universe/God/Creator.

- Give up trying to figure out how or when or where or with whom. Know that your creation will come in a way that you will least expect. It will surprise you and leave no doubt that this came from a higher power.

When you are subconsciously skilled at something, it means you just do it without having to place a great deal of conscious thought or attention to the activity. This is what you want to have happen. You want to practice being the new you so much that it becomes subconscious. The keys to meditation and visualization are to focus on frequency, intensity, and duration. The more you do it, the easier it gets. The better you can focus and concentrate, the easier it will be for you to tap into that particular mindset the next time. The longer you can linger in the thoughts and emotions of your new ideal without letting your mind wander to extraneous stimulus, the more you will memorize new thoughts and feelings.

Creating a New Reality

Your new personality should create a new reality. When you are being someone else, you naturally will have a different life. The new identity is no longer emotionally anchored to known situations in your life that keep recycling the same circumstances; therefore, it is a perfect place from which to envision a new destiny. This is the place you want to be to create your hero life.

The reason your past intensions hardly ever manifested is that you were trying to hold a mindful intention while being lost in lower emotions such as guilt, shame, sadness, unworthiness, anger, or fear connect to the old self. It was those feelings that were governing your thoughts and attitude. The 5 percent of your conscious mind was fighting against the 95 percent of your subconscious. Thinking one way and feeling another cannot produce results.

Creating a New Destiny

Now that you have released that old energy from the body, what do you want? Do you want to heal an area of your body or life? Do you want a loving relationship, a more satisfying career, a new car? Is your dream to write a book, to send your kids to college, or to go back to school yourself? From a new state of mind, body, and gratitude in a greater, more coherent energy, see these images in your mind of what you want to create in your new life. Craft the specific future events you want to experience by observing them into physical reality. You as the quantum observer are commanding matter to conform to your intentions. With clarity you will hold the image of each manifestation in your mind for a few seconds, and the let it go into the quantum field to be executed by your Universe/God/Creator.

Write down what you want now that you are the new you.

1. _____

2. _____

3. _____

4. _____

5. _____

It might be helpful to create six-month goals from this list. By putting dates on when you expect to have or be these new ideas you are giving the quantum field even more information to help it manifest with you. Of course, you still need to be surprised as to how or even when these events will occur. In fact, these areas might be manifested way before your goal date. Again, be as specific as you can be in what you want so you can visualize it and feel the joy and emotion of having achieved it in your life.

You are now ready to start your meditations. Now that you have worked through the transformational ladder, created a new you, and made your six-months goals, it's time to put it all together into one mediation that you can do every day.

Rehearsing the New You—System Overview

This is an overview of the entire medication/visualization method that, when practiced daily, will create the new you with new thoughts, emotions, and behaviors.

Part 1—The Induction Phase

It is time to relax the body and mind. The brain's electrical signals vary depending on what level of relaxation or arousal you are in. Alpha waves are generated when the brain is conscious but relaxed. Theta waves usually occur during sleep but can be induced when in deep meditation. Theta waves are the gateway to learning, memory, and intuition.

Progressive muscle relaxation is a great way to get the mind into alpha or theta waves which are extremely conducive to the power of suggestion. The best way to do this is to do a guided body relaxation meditation. This is essentially what hypnotherapists do.

Part 2—Remind Yourself Who You Don't Want to Be

Once your brain is in alpha or theta, pick one emotion (at a time) and associated thoughts, feelings, actions, and behaviors that you want to be rid of. Remind yourself of the emotions, feelings, and behaviors you use to think and feel and ask the Universe/God/Creator to take this emotion away from you. You can find these lists in your Transformational Ladder exercises.

Part 3—Create the New You

Take what you have answered in the Creating the New You exercises and feel into the new you. How you will think and act. Think about being like this new person. Picture yourself acting, doing, and saying what this new you would say and do.

Part 4—Visualize What the New You Wants

Picture the images in your mind and feel how you would feel with the new areas in your life. What's going on around you? What are people saying or doing with you? Feel the emotion of having and doing this new behavior.

Part 5—Release the Vision

Release your new vision of you to the Universe/God/Creator and ask for a sign that you made a connection.

Part 6—Give Thanks

Give thanks for having or being this new person. Be in so much gratitude and live in that gratitude all day long.

Part 7— Live as If

Live the rest of the day as if you are that new person and have such gratitude for the life you are living as this new person with this new behavior.

SECTION THREE
QUANTUM MEDITATIONS

CHAPTER 9
QUANTUM REPROGRAMMING MEDITATION

Meditation/Visualization

There are various ways to get into an alpha/theta state. A standard breathing meditation can do it for some, while others might need guided progressive muscle relaxation with music to get there.

Here is a simple, guided progressive muscle relaxation meditation that you can use. You can also use any good guided meditation to get into an alpha/theta wave state.

You can download this meditation set to peaceful background music at www.betheheroofyourlife.com/downloads.

Induction

Take a minute to get settled and comfortable in your chair or seated position. Take a few deep breaths to relax. Gently close your eyes and continue to take deep breaths. With your eyes closed, feel into your surroundings. Feel into your body and the places your body touches— the chair or floor. Feel your feet flat on the floor. Feel your seat in the chair and where your back hits the chair. Feel your hands resting on your lap. Now, take a moment to hear any sounds in the room, both inside and out.

Let any cares or worries drift away now as this is your time to relax and be. Now, begin to focus on your breathing as you inhale and exhale. Be with each breath for its full duration. Notice the rise and fall of your chest and stomach with each breath. Now, as you breathe in, feel the air hit the back of your throat and your lungs filling with air. As you breathe out, feel your body soften, releasing any tension. Allow your body to feel more relaxed and more peaceful with each breath. Enjoy the simplicity of this moment. Use your breath to anchor yourself to the present moment. Now, bring your attention to your face and feel any tension, and let it dissolve. Be aware of your head and notice the tiny muscles around your eyes and feel any tension drift away. Now, focus on your jaw, allowing it to relax with your teeth apart, releasing any tension.

Now, move your awareness to your shoulders and into your upper arms, your elbows, forearms, and wrists. Sense the back of your hands, your palm, and your fingers.

Now, draw your attention to the back of the shoulders, following the arch from your upper back down to your lower back and to your hips. Allow the earth below your feet to draw you down into a grounded sensation. You feel grounded and centered.

Move your focus now to your thighs and down to your knees, your calf muscles, your shins, ankles and feet, down to your heels and to your toes, and all the way to the tips of your toes. Just relax. You feel centered and balanced.

Now, focus your awareness on your body as a whole and rest for a moment. You're feeling very safe and secure now. Sense the energy field around your entire body. You may even sense its vibration and color. As you focus on your whole body and your energy field, acknowledge any feelings or sensations as they come into your being. Imagine any tension, fear, or stress dissolving away. Just letting go.

Now, I want you to imagine sitting near a gentle stream on a beautiful, warm summer's day. There is lush green grass all around you, and you feel a pleasant and refreshing breeze against your skin as you enjoy these beautiful surroundings. If you ever had any fears of water, they fade away now. This is a magical healing place, a place where you feel safe and secure and at peace. Listen to the sound of the trickling stream as the sun sparkles on the surface of the water. The sound of trickling water fascinates you. It brings your awareness to the present moment. It feels like time is standing still.

As you continue to gaze at the water, you watch the gentle ebb and flow of the stream. Notice a few leaves floating on the surface of the water. As you watch the leaves moving slowly down the stream, notice any thoughts that may enter your mind. As they enter, mentally place each thought on a single leaf. As they come into your awareness, place your thoughts onto the leaves, one at a time. Then, watch as they pass by, float along the stream, and out of view. It doesn't matter if they are happy or sad thoughts or where they came from; simply acknowledge them and let them go. Simply relax and just be in the present moment. If a thought comes into your mind, simply place it on a leaf and watch it flow downstream and out of sight.

Long pause here.

Now, drift away in a state of blissful presence and the gentle sounds will continue to wash over you. You feel completely refreshed and relaxed and have a deep sense of peace and well-being.

Now that you are totally relaxed and in alpha state, gently transition into the next part of the meditation.

Declare the Emotions You Want to Change and Remind Yourself Who You No Longer Want to Be

Say the emotions you want to change out loud and free them from your body, as well as your environment. Say them now.

Make sure that no thought, behavior, or feeling can cause you to return to the old self. Remember how you used to think when you felt that way? What did you say to yourself? What voice did you listen to that you no longer want to accept as your reality? Observe those thoughts. How did you once behave? How did you speak? Become conscious of these subconscious states to such an extent that they will never go unnoticed by you again.

Remind yourself who you no longer want to be, how you no longer want to think, how you no longer want to behave, and how you no longer want to feel. Become familiar with all aspects of the old personality, and just observe. With firm intention, make a choice to no longer be that person, and let the energy of your decisions become a memorable experience.

Create the New You

Now that you absolutely know what you want to change, let's create the new hero of your life.

What is the greatest expression of yourself that you can be? How would you, as this great person, think and act? How will you live? How will you love? What does greatness feel like? Move into a new state of being. It is time to change your energy and broadcast a whole new electromagnetic signature. When you change your energy, you change your life. Let your thoughts become the experience, and let that experience produce elevated emotions so that your body begins to emotionally believe that the future you is already living now.

Allow yourself to fall in love with the new ideal you; open your heart and begin to recondition your body to a new mind.

Let the inward experience become a mood, then a temperament, and finally a new personality. Move into a new state of being. Do not get up as the same person who sat down. You must feel gratitude so that your body begins to change ahead of the actual event, and accept that the new ideal already is you. Become it. Empowered, to be free, unlimited, creative, genius, divine—this is who you are.

Once you feel this way, memorize this feeling; remember this feeling. This is who you truly are.

Now let go and release it into the unlimited quantum field for a moment. Just let go.

You must wire that new mind again and recondition the body to a new emotion. What's the greatest expression of yourself? Allow yourself to begin to think like this ideal you again.

What would you say to yourself, how would you walk, how would you breathe, how would you move, how would you live, what would you feel? Allow yourself to emotionally feel like this new self, so much that you begin to move into a new state of being.

Who do you want to be when you open your eyes? Feel empowered once again. This is where you create a new destiny. From this elevated state of mind and body, it is time to command matter. As a quantum creator of your new reality, feel invincible, powerful, inspired, grateful, and overjoyed.

From this new state of being, form a picture of some event you want to experience and let the images become the reality of your future. Observe that reality and allow the particles as waves of probability collapse into an event or experience in your life. See it, command it, hold it, and then move to the next image.

That future event must find you because you created it with your own energy. Let yourself go and create the future you want in certainty, trust, and knowingness. Do not analyze or try to figure out how it is going to happen. It is not your job to control the outcome. It is your task to design your ideal self and leave the details to the Universe/God/ Creator. As you see your future as the observer, simply bless your life with your own energy. From a state of gratitude, be one with your destiny. Give thanks for a new life.

Feel how you will feel when these things manifest in your life because living in a state of gratitude is living in a state of feeling blessed. Feel like your prayers are already answered. Finally, it's time to turn to that power within you and ask it for a sign in your life. If today you connected to this Universe/God/Creator mind, observed all of life into form, and made contact with it, then it has been observing your efforts and intentions and should show up in your life. Know that it is real, that it exists, and that you now have a two-way communication with it. Ask that this sign from the Universe/God/Creator come in a way that you would least expect; in a way that surprises you and leaves you with no doubt that this new experience has come from the Universe/ God/Creator. Ask for a sign now.

Now, go and live the rest of your day as if you are that new person and be grateful for the life you are living as this new person.

Now, move your awareness back to a new body in a new environment and in a whole new line of time. And when you are ready, bring your awareness back to your body. Then you can open your eyes.

Congratulations! What a journey you've taken. You have put your life into the 12 stages of the hero's journey and followed your bliss. You have identified your limiting beliefs, thoughts, and emotions and redirected them. And finally, you started the anchoring process to create the new you and get to the place where your purpose is guiding you.

Even though you've come a long way, worked very hard, and faced your fears, the real work is just beginning. Now that you've identified what you don't want to be anymore and the hero you want to become, you have to do your meditation/visualization practice every day for at least three months and then add to it or change it. The power is in consistency—you must train your brain to prune away the old neural networks and create new ones. You will also need to continuously create a coherent high mental frequency so the Universe/God/Creator knows you are serious and will open up and work with you on your dreams.

It is my sincere hope that you find inspiration in this process and take from it what you need. I hope you let your hero's journey guide you to follow your bliss and find your life purpose. Your life purpose doesn't need to be your job or career. It can be anything that adds to the well-being of others. That's the real magic of finding your purpose. When you do this, you will jump out of bed in the morning excited to use your gifts to help others and make a difference. As Joseph Campbell says, following your bliss and finding your life purpose is the essence of the hero's journey. If you follow just this one concept you will make a difference and create a life of purpose, joy, and fulfillment.

Good luck.

SECTION FOUR
APPENDICES

APPENDIX A
EXERCISES

EXERCISE 1
YOUR LIFE TIMELINE

Complete a timeline of your life up until now. List the most significant events. This isn't a detailed list of your whole life, but it will give you a good idea of where you are in the twelve stages of the hero's journey exercise below.

Example Timeline

Year	Life Event
1962	Born in Helena, Montana
1980	Graduated from Flathead High School
1986	Graduated from University of Montana with a psychology degree
1987	Packed up my Honda Civic and drove across the country to start my life in Washington, DC
1987	Got my first real job at Tymnet—living in Northern Virginia
1989	Got married
...	...

Your Turn:

Year	Life Event

EXERCISE 2
PREPARATION PHASE

Reread the first four stages of the Preparation phase of the hero's journey. Then place your life events into each stage. Make sure to identify not only what was going on in your life at this time but what this time in your life meant to you. Don't worry if you can't identify a part of your life that doesn't fit into a particular stage. You can skip it or come back to it later.

Decide as early in the process as you can if you are going to list out your entire life until now into one big hero's journey or you think you may have had more than one already. Remember that you can have multiple events in your life that may be in one stage. For example, you may have had many calls to adventure but refused the call many times before actually crossing the threshold. I find it helpful to try and fit a large chunk of life into one hero's journey. You may, and usually will, find that you are in the middle of your hero's journey with a few stages yet to move through.

Stage One: The Ordinary World

Try to remember a time in your life when you were living your life and seemingly things were fine, but you felt a small inkling that something wasn't quite right and there was something more out there for you. Detail the date and time in your life and describe what was going on in your life then.

Example:

I was living in suburbia with my two kids and my wife. I was working my ass off to get ahead and make a good life for my family. I wasn't exercising or eating a good diet, and I was becoming miserable. I began to think something in my life had to change.

Your Turn:

_____

_____

_____

Stage Two: The Call to Adventure

Now that you have established your ordinary world, follow through your timeline to when something happened in your life that woke you up and got your attention. This could be a hardship like a job loss, divorce, or loss of a loved one, or it could be that you just woke up one day and knew you had to make a change in your life.

Example:

I was in the shower when I heard a voice say, "This is not the way to live your life—you must be doing something wrong."

Your Turn:

_____

_____

_____

Stage Three: Refusal of the Call

Describe a time in your life when you heard the call to adventure but were too afraid or confused to follow through and make a change in your life.

Example:

I repeatedly refused the call. After I heard the call in the shower that morning it would be another nine years before I would fully answer the call, enter my new world by getting a divorce, leaving a job of 16 years, and starting my own business.

Your Turn:

_____

_____

_____

Stage Four: Meeting with the Mentor

Who has been a mentor to you in your life? Mentors can be people you admired or learned from either before your call to adventure or after. As you progress through your journey you may lean on these mentors heavily or acquire new ones.

Example:

Through the years, I've hired many therapists and coaches to help me move through the stuck times in life or to help boost my businesses. I've also gleaned a great deal of wisdom from books or seminars I have attended to aid me on my journey.

Your Turn:

_____

_____

_____

_____

_____

_____

_____

EXERCISE 3
IS YOUR EGO PREPARED
FOR THE JOURNEY?

The following questions will help you determine what Preparation stage you need help with or what events should fit into a certain stage.

- What calls for change are presenting themselves to you right now?

_____

- Are there calls from your past that you have ignored or refused? Do they still call out to you?

_____

- To whom did you look for direction when you were growing up?

_____

- Are there others who acted directly or indirectly as teachers or coaches?

_____

- Would life be different if you hadn't met your mentors?

_____

Now that you have completed your Preparation phase stages, answer the following questions to help you decide if your ego has progressed in a developmentally healthy way. Don't be critical if you still need work in this area. Most of us do.

- Do you find yourself continuously doing things so others will like you or think you are okay?

- Do you have a hard time delegating? Do you feel you must run everything by yourself?

- Do you have a hard time accepting other people's wishes or truths even if they conflict with yours?

- Are you afraid to say what you think because someone might get angry, or are you afraid to leave a relationship or a job for fear that you can't make it on your own?

- Do you have a hard time accepting constructive criticism?

- Are you taking care of everyone in your family or office except yourself?

These answers should allow you to pinpoint areas that you may need to continue to work on before or as you move into the Journey and Return phases. They may also show you areas that you might want to change or add to your above stages.

THE JOURNEY

Stage Five: Crossing the Threshold

Review your timeline and find the time in your life where you finally said, enough with this old way of thinking or living! and actually made a change in your life. You were finally able to move out of your comfort zone and start something new or end something that needed ending, and it changed your life in a new direction. If you can't think of a time when you feel you've crossed the threshold, then maybe you are still refusing the call in your ordinary life. That's okay. Try and imagine a future timeline for your hero's journey and use it as a catalyst to move forward in your life.

Example:

My initial crossing the threshold came after I said to hell with all the doctors and physical therapists. At this point, I wasn't sure what to do other than try to chill out.

Your Turn:

_____

_____

_____

_____

Stage Six: Tests, Allies, and Enemies

Now that you've crossed the threshold and are living in the new, unfamiliar, special world, identify any trials and tribulations you went through as you moved through this new and unfamiliar territory. List friends and allies that appeared during this time who helped you get through them. Also list or describe any enemies that you needed to face down. Enemies can also be difficult situations that you had to overcome.

Example:

After my divorce I started a new career as a professional portrait photographer. Now that all my old familiar friends from the marriage and my work were gone, I had to go out and meet new friends and make new allies.

Your Turn:

_____

_____

_____

_____

_____

_____

Stage Seven: The Approach

Define a time in your life when you went into planning or strengthening or learning mode. This is a time in your life where you were in the thick of life. You are living in the new world and preparing to grow stronger—physically, emotionally, or both. You may not have known it at the time but you were preparing for even harder times ahead. This can be a very good time in your life when you felt like you were alive because you were moving forward.

Example:

As my consulting business was taking off, I started to focus on my body, and I began eating healthier and exercising more. I even went on a grain-free diet and lost 40 pounds.

Your Turn:

_____

_____

_____

Stage Eight: The Ordeal

Describe a time in your life where you had to face a situation scarier than anything you had encountered before. Detail what it was, what you went through, and the insights it brought. There may be more than one ordeal that comes to mind. Just pick one at this time that fits with your timeline and hero's journey so far. There will be other times in your journey where you will undergo trials and tribulations and have to face dragons and ogres, and you can list them then.

Example:

This stage for me was very long and painful. I have identified two parts of my life where I faced uphill battles and have named these my "dark days."

Your Turn:

_____

_____

_____

_____

_____

EXERCISE 5
IS YOUR SOUL PREPARED FOR THE RETURN?

Now that you have completed the Journey phase, it is time to reflect. Remember times when you felt satisfied or curious or content and allowed yourself to be fully present with all the sensations and images that fed your desires. As you build momentum along your journey, you can also allow your fantasies to soar. Ask the following questions of yourself gently and repeat each question or answer each prompt until you are satisfied with your answer. For example: "I like ____. Another thing I like is _____." Don't edit or critique your answers. Answer each question with the first words that pop into your head.

- I like _____.
- I feel satisfied when _____.
- I fully enjoy _____.
- I want to do more _____.
- I am happy when I _____.
- What dreams do I have, day or night, that reveal my purpose? _____ _____.
- I feel fulfilled when I _____.

- I feel curious about_____.
- If I could change anything in my life I would change
  _____.
- In my wildest fantasies, I have always wanted to ____
  _____.
- My gifts, talents, and strengths include _____
  _____.

Now, review your list and decide which of these you can pass on to others.

- Of all my gifts, talents, and strengths, which is my best, the one that makes me stand out?
  _____.
- Am I willing to give up the life I've planned so I can have the life that is waiting for me?
  _____.
- Where in my life am I playing defense? What would it look like to play some offense?
  _____.
- One thing that I will do today that scares me is ____
  _____.

These answers should allow you to pinpoint areas that you may need to continue to work on before you can move into the Return phase.

EXERCISE 6
RETURN PHASE

Stage Nine: The Reward

Identify a time in your life when you crossed the threshold, faced hardships (dragons) that you overcame, and claimed victory. Be aware though, that there will be at least one more challenge to face on your journey home with the reward.

Example:

In October of the year I was diagnosed, I was declared cancer free. I had conquered my fearful ordeal and won the battle with cancer. I was back on track, living my life, and consulting in Kansas.

Your Turn:

_____

_____

_____

Stage Ten: The Road Back

This is a critical stage because you must return home after the victory. Remember a time in your life where you had achieved victory and were on the road back home to the ordinary world. Again, you will still be tested further before reaching home.

Example:

At this stage in my life, the only chase scene I was experiencing was my dating failures. I was chasing my tail trying to find true love again. I was trying various ways to find my girlfriend, from meetups to online dating to hanging out in bars with no success stories.

Your Turn:

_____

_____

_____

Stage Eleven: The Resurrection

This may be the most interesting stage in the journey. It was for me, at least. Just when you think you have defeated your dragons and claimed victory on your way home, you are severely tested one more time. Think of a time in your life when after a victory you were tested or faced one more challenge that purified you with one last lesson. Remember that even though this challenge may be the most severe, you have been on your hero's journey and have gained valuable insights, skills, and mentors to help you face this last challenge.

Example:

I had been dating on and off since returning to Kansas, but nothing was even remotely serious until one day out of the blue I met a woman who would profoundly change the course of my life.

Your Turn:

_____

_____

_____

Stage Twelve: Return with the Treasure

You finally made it back to your ordinary world with treasure in hand. You have gained much insight and strength during your journey. Your reward is either something tangible, like a new job, a relationship, renewed health—or even more likely—an amazing story of survival to tell your tribe. Describe a time where you found your true, authentic self and were living your life purpose.

Example:

As I mentioned, this book is part of my Return phase. Completing my hero's journey opened a whole new avenue of creativity for me. During my journey I encountered many mentors and healers and through meditation and journaling I realized that I have always had a sense to help people through education.

Your Turn:

EXERCISE 7
HAVE YOU FOUND YOURSELF?

These questions will help you decide if you have completed your journey or not.

- What is my personal kingdom, and what are my responsibilities to myself?

_____

_____

_____

_____

_____

_____

_____

- What are my responsibilities to other people?

_____

_____

_____

_____

_____

_____

_____

_____

- Write a description of your role and responsibilities in the following areas of life:
- family
- primary relationship
- work
- church or community group

_____

_____

_____

_____

_____

_____

_____

_____

_____

- Is it your turn to give back and pay it forward? Are you prepared to be a mentor?

_____

_____

_____

_____

_____

_____

_____

_____

EXERCISE 8
HERO'S JOURNEY SUMMARY

Now that you have broken down your life according to the stages of the hero's journey it's time to put it all together and draw some conclusions. You want to figure out where in your life you have been the hero that was called to adventure, where you battled your metaphorical dragons and came out the victor. You also want to know where you refused the call. See if you can figure out why you refused the call for so long before you had the courage to cross the threshold and take your journey. What finally gave you the courage to move forward? Do you still have that courage today or have you lost it somehow?

Review all of your stages and put together a few paragraphs of what you have gleaned by sorting your life into stages of the hero's journey. If you get on a roll and find yourself writing pages and pages, by all means go for it. This can be a very cathartic and eye-opening experience. I know it was for me.

 In later exercises you will be identifying your limiting stories, beliefs, and behaviors. You will want to use your hero's journey story to help identify those.

Example:

I started my adult life full of hope and passion. I wanted to live the American dream of owning a house in the suburbs, enjoying time with my wife, and watching my kids grow up. What I didn't realize is that I was predisposed to general anxiety disorder and as I pursued the dream I was piling on heaps of stress and secreting stress-producing hormones that were taking a toll on my body. Basically, I was in flight or fight all the time and the human body isn't made to function that way.

My hero's journey started when I heard the call to adventure in the shower one morning. But unfortunately, it would be more than nine years before I would accept the call and cross the threshold into the unknown world. My wakeup call was getting laid off and divorced in the span of one year. The Universe knocked me on my ass.

I struggled for years in the unknown world, drinking too much and feeling lonely, and then getting cancer. But I rallied and healed and made a comeback by helping others and writing about my experiences in life.

After I returned from my journey and claimed victory, I took up the mantle of mentor, wrote this book, and started life coaching to help people with life's challenges and to help them move forward as I did.

As this journey ends I embark on a new hero's journey, refining my purpose, building my business, and fostering new relationships.

Your Turn:

_____

_____

_____

_____

_____

_____

_____

_____

_____

_____

_____

_____

_____

THE
TRANSFORMATIONAL
LADDER

No matter if you are stuck in the middle of your hero's journey or have completed many hero's journeys, there is always room for improvement. Human suffering comes from the illusion that we are not enough. This is universal for humans and it starts in young childhood when we are completely at the mercy of our parents to support us in life.

The transformational ladder will guide you from defining your limiting behaviors down through the limiting stories you tell yourself and what emotions are causing the main limiting beliefs that were created by original life-triggering events. With this information, you will be ready to move on to climbing back up the ladder with new empowering beliefs, emotions, stories, and behaviors and become the hero of your life.

The exercises below will help you figure out where you are stuck in life and will give you insight on how to get unstuck and move forward in your journey. If you have completed the exercises in Section One on the hero's journey, you can already see how your life has unfolded into your journey. Now it's time to go deep and define what you want to change in your life and why. It's your job to look back on your life and figure out where things may have gone wrong or where unfortunate circumstances took place and what meaning you attached to those life events. As you use the exercises to uncover your personal growth pattern, you will begin to see yourself as the hero of your own life and how your life has shaped your journey so far. With this knowledge, you will peel back the onion of your transformational ladder and sit with this knowledge for a while. With a clear understanding of how your past life might have contributed to your limiting beliefs and actions, you will rebuild your ideal hero life.

Uncovering Where You Are Stuck

The first step to change is admitting you are stuck. Where are you stuck in your life? These are areas where you are most frustrated, annoyed, disappointed, feeling helpless. The primary feelings of being stuck are powerlessness, hiding, and frustration. Some examples might be:

- You are stuck in a relationship you know isn't working.

- You are stuck in a job that is sucking the life out of you.

- You have lost your connection to your faith.

- You never have enough money.

- You are overweight.

- You are out of shape.

- Your family doesn't support you.

- You have chronic pain.

List where you feel you are stuck:

1. _____

2. _____

3. _____

4. _____

5. _____

Now take a few minutes to reflect on these stuck areas of your life above by answering the following questions.

How have you ignored these stuck areas or used them as excuses?

_____

_____

_____

How long have these stuck areas been with you? Are you repeating a pattern?

_____

_____

_____

Can you remember the first time you felt stuck in these areas?

_____

_____

_____

Do you believe that staying stuck in these areas benefited you in any way?

_____

_____

_____

Do you have any relationships in your life that support you being stuck in these areas?

_____

_____

Why Must You Change?

Let's get clear on why you must change. What have you missed out on because you let fear and apathy rule your life? List your missed opportunities below.

- **Romance:**
  - _____

- **Career:**
  - _____

- **Health:**
  - _____

- **Spirituality:**
  - _____

- **Relationships:**
  - _____

- **Finances:**
  - _____

- **Volunteering:**
  - _____

- **Add Your Own Category** _____:
  - _____

Make a list of all the things you want in your life. What do you want to feel? What do you want to do with your life? What things do you want to have in your life? Whom do you want to love?

1. _____

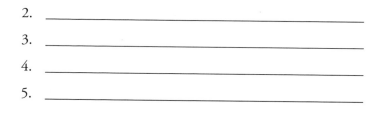

2. _____

3. _____

4. _____

5. _____

Write out why you must commit to changing now (be as detailed as possible).

_____

_____

_____

_____

- **What is the worst that could happen if you don't change now?**

  - _____

  - _____

- **What's the worst thing that could happen if you decide to change now?**

  - _____

  - _____

- **Has the Universe/God/Creator tried to get your attention recently? What were the signs?**

  - _____

  - _____

Now that you have identified where you are stuck, why you must change, and what you want out of life, you will dive into your emotions and what limiting beliefs, stories, and events have held you back.

What differentiates between a belief, an emotion, a story, and a behavior in this context? When you have an early trauma or crisis in your life, a belief is the meaning that you created from that traumatic event. Beliefs create emotions or a felt sense in the body. Your emotions create your stories or how you describe your circumstances. Your stories create your behaviors or how you repeatedly react to your circumstances.

We are wired to assign meaning to what happens to us in life. The amazing thing, though, is that no one else can assign meaning to our life events. Only we can do that. That should make you feel very hopeful.

Your Limiting Stories, Beliefs, Emotions, Thinking, and Behaviors

Our behaviors are usually driven by the stories we tell ourselves. We don't just do things randomly. Our thoughts create our behavior. Every behavior was first a thought or story.

Identifying Your Limiting Stories

- There are all kinds of stories that hold you back. Common ones are:
- The world is not a safe place.
- I'm too old.
- I'm too fat.
- I don't have enough time.
- I don't have enough money.
- I'm too young.
- Life will never get better.
- This is all I'm worth.

- I've always been this way.
- I don't feel I can be my true self.
- My children's happiness is more important than my own.
- My parents don't approve of who I am.
- Life doesn't support me.
- I'm cursed.
- This works for other people but not for me.

What stories are you telling yourself? Write them down.

1. _____

2. _____

3. _____

4. _____

5. _____

Where Did Your Limiting Stories Come From?

As you ask yourself where your limiting stories come from, remember not to beat yourself up. Be kind and gentle with yourself as you look at the hard parts of your life and trust the process. Go back and read what you wrote about the stories you tell yourself. Allow yourself to soak them in. Don't push them away. Then ask yourself, did I hear these stories from someone else first? Consider these influential sources:

- parents
- significant others
- religious leaders
- bosses

- brothers or sisters
- the media
- bullies in school
- friends
- extended family members
- role models

Try and think about the actual words that these people said to you. Common examples are:

- Finish what's on your plate; there are starving kids in India.
- You'll never amount to anything.
- You're going to be just like your mother/father.
- Children should be seen and not heard.
- No one in this family has ever gone to college. What makes you think you can?
- Don't air your dirty laundry in public.

List the top five times when you first heard these limiting stories and what they were.

1. _____

2. _____

3. _____

4. _____

5. _____

Identifying Your Limiting Beliefs

Beliefs are in many ways the origin of the stories we tell about life. Beliefs are more powerful than stories because beliefs are based on the meaning we gave past events in our lives. In other words, belief determines how we see or perceive events. Like a filter. And a story is the account of what happened or what will happen based on your beliefs. Some examples are:

- I'll never get a new job.

- No one ever listens to me.

- He always makes me feel angry.

- Everyone uses me.

- I want to call it quits.

- Today is a bad day for me, so why bother trying to change it.

- It's her fault that my life is this way.

- I'm really not that smart.

- I honestly can't change. Maybe it would be better to start another time.

- I don't feel like it.

- My life sucks.

- I hate my situation with _____.

- I'll never make a difference. I can't.

- _____ does not like me.

- I have to work harder than most people.

- It's my genetics. I am just like my mother/father.

Review the stories you tell yourself and where they came from and turn them into belief statements. List your limiting beliefs here:

1. _____

2. _____

3. _____

4. _____

5. _____

Identifying Your Limiting Emotions

Go back to the list you created of the limiting thinking, stories, and beliefs that hold you back. Reread them. Then bring your awareness to your body. How are you feeling as you read these stories, thoughts, and beliefs, and where are you feeling it? Some people feel these deep strong emotions in their stomachs or jaws. Others feel them manifest as weakness in their legs. Pay attention to where you feel them.

Right now we are just going to sit with those feelings rather than acting on them. If this brings up panic, fear, and shame, that is okay. There is nothing wrong with you. Remember, you are not your feelings and emotions.

I usually feel my deep emotions in my throat and solar plexus. Where do you feel your deep emotions?

Think of all the times your limiting stories, thoughts, and beliefs have held you back. Look at the pain you've caused others. Look at the pain you've caused yourself. Look how you have kept yourself small, how you've put others first and denied your own worth and intuition. Look back over your hero's journey life and see how you've held yourself back. Notice how this makes you feel and where you feel it in your body.

Naming Your Emotions

Now that you have gotten in touch with your emotions, list five emotions that you feel as a result of these limiting behaviors and stories and the areas in your body where you feel them.

If it is hard to access your emotions, or if you're getting frustrated that you aren't feeling anything, this is good. You're feeling frustrated. Where do you feel that in your body? Just because you don't feel the emotions you think you should be feeling doesn't mean you can't feel. Your job is to go with whatever is present in the here and now. Some common emotions are:

- anger
- hate
- powerlessness
- guilt
- shame
- sadness
- unworthiness
- betrayal
- regret
- depression
- stress
- self-doubt
- lack of belonging
- resentment

List your emotions and where you feel them in your body.

I feel _____ in my _____.

I feel _____ in my _____.

I feel _____ in my _____.

I feel _____ in my _____.

I feel _____ in my _____.

These are difficult things to feel, and you may want to turn back, but don't. Stay with them. These feelings will pass and fade away. These emotions do not control you. In fact, feeling them is the first step toward setting yourself free.

Identify Your Limiting Thinking

Next ask yourself: How do I think when I feel this way? For example, if you want to get rid of the feeling of shame, ask yourself: What is my attitude when I feel shame? You might say you are scared or timid or quiet and shy. An attitude is a series of thoughts connected to a feeling. You need to define the habit that has been created by these emotions. You may develop attitudes that are:

- competitive
- blaming
- desperate
- overly intellectual
- lazy
- dishonest
- controlling
- needy

- sensitive
- insensitive

List your own top five attitudes.

1. _____

2. _____

3. _____

4. _____

5. _____

Most of your actions, behaviors, and choices have made you act in predictable ways. Right now, consider these emotional attitudes without doing anything. Just observe them.

Identifying Your Limiting Behaviors

Your stories create your behaviors or how you repeatedly react to your circumstances. What behaviors do you blame yourself for doing and yet can't seem to find a way past?

Some of these behaviors might be:

- self-sabotage
- overeating
- blaming others
- withdrawing or hiding
- lying
- abusing porn
- abusing gambling
- cheating on your partner

List your limiting behaviors here:

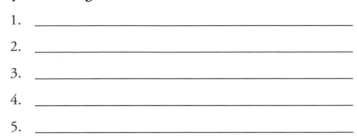

1. _____

2. _____

3. _____

4. _____

5. _____

Uncovering Your Triggering Life Events

We are going to go back to a time of hurt—a time you have pushed away for so long, a time that you may even have pretended didn't happen and that you don't want to talk about. It is your moment or moments of trauma, pain, and original hurt.

These triggering life events are moments in our past when something happened and we decided to form beliefs about the world. They come from all kinds of places. They can be something as simple as being left behind at school, a kid calling you fat, or the tone in which a parent said something to you as a child. Or they could be more extreme, like sexual, emotional, or physical abuse.

The majority of these triggering life events start before the age of 10. Because they are never addressed or worked through, these limiting beliefs carry themselves into adulthood. In order to change your story these triggering life events must be seen with new eyes. It's time to uncover how you created these limiting beliefs to protect yourself long ago. It may take running through this process a few times to find all the triggering life events. Common triggering life events include:

- sexual abuse

- physical abuse

- emotional abuse

- violent family members
- being required to be perfect, rather than yourself
- being abandoned by one or both parents
- a parent's addiction
- needing to be the caregiver of your parent as a child
- other people condemning you
- being made fun of at school
- witnessing violence
- the death of a loved one
- not being recognized by your father
- not being nurtured by your mother

Go back and read your top five limiting beliefs. Take a minute to let the emotions to wash over you.

Now list the triggering life events that shaped your beliefs.

1. _____
2. _____
3. _____
4. _____
5. _____

Admitting Who You Are

Acknowledge your true self rather than the self you show to other people. Allow yourself to be vulnerable. Tell the Universe/God/ Creator who you have been and what you want to change about yourself and admit what you are hiding.

Owning up to who we really are, what our past mistakes have been, and asking to be accepted are among the most challenging things for us to do as humans. This works because we are admitting our faults and failures to our higher power and not to another similarly flawed human.

Close your eyes and become still and begin to tell this higher power who you have been. Share the details of the stories that you have carried around with you. Some examples might be:

- I am afraid of falling in love because it hurts too much.

- I pretend I am happy, but I am really suffering because I am lonely.

- I do not want anyone to know that I feel so guilty, so I lie about myself.

- I lie to people so that they like me and so I won't feel unloved and unworthy.

- I can't stop feeling self-pity. I think, act, and feel this way all day long because I do not know how else I can feel.

- I have felt like a failure most of my life, so I try extra to be a success.

Write down what comes up for you.

_____

_____

_____

_____

_____

Creating the New You—Climbing Back up the Transformational Ladder

Up until now you've worked at identifying your limited thinking and pruning away old synaptic connections. Now it's time to sprout new ones so that the new mind you create will become the platform for who you will be in your future. Let's find your bliss and create a new you. Your daily meditations, contemplations, and rehearsals will be like tending to a garden to yield a great expression of the new you. You should fall in love with the vision of who you are becoming. Love is a higher frequency emotion than those in survival emotions that allowed the negative and limiting beliefs to control your subconscious thinking.

In the 2006 movie, *The Pursuit of Happyness,* directed by Gabriele Muccino, Will Smith stars as Chris Gardner, a person who has everything go wrong in his life. The film shows that even someone with these misfortunes can succeed by never giving up. Chris Gardner continues to tell himself and everyone around him that he will succeed and be able to provide for his son. My favorite scene from the movie is when Chris is talking to his son on the basketball court.

"Don't ever let someone tell you that you can't do something," he says. "Not even me. You got a dream? You got to protect it. People can't do something themselves they want to tell you, you can't do it. You want something, go get it. Period."

Focus on the positive, redirect your negative self-talk to positive, and never give up. This is how heroes live and return with the treasure of a purpose-driven and fulfilling life.

Below are a series of open-ended questions that will cause you to think in different ways than you normally think and to entertain new possibilities. This turns on your frontal lobe. You are creating the platform of the new self by forcing the brain to fire in novel ways.

Write down answers to as many questions as seem relevant to you. After you complete the answers, review, reflect, analyze and think about all the possibilities your answers raise. You will then be climbing the transformational ladder with new beliefs, emotions, stories, and behaviors.

How Do I Want to Think?

- What is my ideal self?

    - _____

    - _____

- What historical figures do I admire?

    - _____

    - _____

- After whom do I want to model my own behavior? How would I be if I were like them?

    - _____

    - _____

- What would I say to myself if I were this new person I want to be?

    - _____

    - _____

How Do I Want to Act?

- How would the "new me" act?

    - _____

    - _____

- What would I do? How do I see myself behaving?

  - _____
  - _____

- How would I talk to others if I were changed?

  - _____
  - _____

- What would my new attitude be?

  - _____
  - _____

- What do I want to believe about the new me?

  - _____
  - _____

- How do I want to be perceived?

  - _____
  - _____

- What would I say to myself if I were this person?

  - _____
  - _____

- How would this person act?

  - _____
  - _____

- How Do I Want to Feel?

  - _____

  - _____

- What would I feel if I were my ideal self?

  - _____

  - _____

- What would my energy be like as this new ideal?

  - _____

  - _____

Now that you have brainstormed how you want to think, feel, and act differently, it's time to get specific on your new empowering stories, beliefs, thinking, and behaviors. Review your limiting stories, beliefs, thinking, and behaviors and rewrite them into positives statements.

What Are the Stories That Will Move You Forward?

List five new, empowering stories that will move you forward.

1. _____

2. _____

3. _____

4. _____

5. _____

What Are the Beliefs That Will Move You Forward?

1. _____

2. _____

3. _____

4. _____

5. _____

List five new, empowering beliefs that will move you forward.

1. _____

2. _____

3. _____

4. _____

5. _____

What New, Empowering Thinking Will Move You Forward?

1. _____

2. _____

3. _____

4. _____

5. _____

List five new, empowering thoughts that will move you forward.

1. _____

2. _____

3. _____

4. _____

5. _____

What Behaviors Will Move You Forward?

1. _____

2. _____

3. _____

4. _____

5. _____

List five new, empowering stories that will move you forward.

1. _____

2. _____

3. _____

4. _____

5. _____

Your Hero Life Moment

Step 1: What Is Your Hero Moment?

Imagine a time in your life when you accomplished or did something that made you feel absolutely incredible. A time where you felt empowered, confident, happy, and full of energy. A time in your life when you felt like you could do anything you put your mind to. It can be *any* time in your life. When you were a kid hitting a home run, acing a test, leaving your job, getting a big check, accomplishing something significant, falling in love, speaking on stage, or doing something you had never done before and crushing it.

_____

_____

_____

Step 2: What Was the Most Powerful Part of Your Hero Life Moment?

_____

_____

_____

Redefine the idea. Pinpoint it all the way down to one specific moment. For examples, pride upon receiving an award, the feeling of crossing home plate after the game-winning home run, the sound of the crowd during a standing ovation, the feeling of looking at an "A" on your final exam.

Step 3: Why Is that Moment so Significant for You?

_____

_____

_____

Attach meaning to it. What does it mean to you? For example, perhaps you accomplished something great before and now you know you can do it again. Or you stepped outside your comfort zone and believe you can do it again. You can do anything if you put your mind to it.

_____

_____

_____

Step 4: Physiologically, How Did You Feel During Your Hero Moment?

What did you feel, how did you stand, how were you breathing, what did you hear?

If you can have that happen to you back then, what is holding you back now? What if you could achieve something this amazing now?

What if you thought about this moment every day and recreated that physiological response in your body? You can leverage this for any project, event, or anytime you want to get pumped up empowered to take action.

Discovering Your Purpose and Passion

Passion and purpose are similar but distinct. They are connected and seductive to us all.

The following exercises will help draw out the purpose and passion that resides within you. Don't come at this with preconceived ideas of what your purpose is or should be or what others think it should be.

Take your time with these questions. The answers you seek will be revealed when you go inward with calmness, patience, and vulnerability.

Think about what makes you tear up.

- When you are emotionally moved, it is a sign of what resonates within you, either good or bad, happy or sad. We all have something that triggers our emotions and feelings. Describe what that is for you.

_____

_____

_____

_____

_____

_____

- **What makes you angry and annoyed?**

  - What kinds of things make you really mad and sometimes push you over the top?

  - When you declare what makes you angry you are leaving clues as to what you are passionate about.

_____

_____

_____

What charges and recharges you?

  - What inspires and motivates you?

  - Is it nature? Is it when you are being creative? Do you like working in groups or by yourself? Does music inspire you? What kind?

  - The answers to this question are closely connected to your purpose and passion.

_____

_____

_____

What are you better at than anyone else you know?

  - This is when you are in your flow zone and quite often lose track of them when you're doing this.

_____

_____

_____

_____

What can people count on you to always do?

- This is where you walk your talk and find it easy to do.
- People have been telling you this your whole life.
- At work, what are you the go-to person for?
- In your family, what is it that you always do?

_____

_____

_____

When will you be worthy?

- What needs to happen for you to feel truly worthwhile? Remember we are hardest on ourselves.

_____

_____

_____

- How will you know when you have "arrived?" When will your credibility be irrefutable?

_____

_____

_____

What gift will you share with the world?

- Your gift may be connected to your deepest desires.

_____

_____

_____

Who or what would you die for?

- What means the most to you? Who would you make the ultimate sacrifice for?

- When you know what you would die for it grants you the wisdom of knowing what to live for.

- Think about what's in it for you.

_____

_____

_____

When your time is up what would your final wish be?

- How will you use it?

- What will it be for?

- Who will benefit?

- When all you have is one wish left, your answer will be very revealing. Your purpose and passion are rooted in your values. You're not allowed to ask for more time.

_____

_____

_____

How do you want to be remembered?

- When you think about this, what would honor your memory the most?

- What stories would you most like to hear told about you at your funeral?

- The answers to this question are what are most important to you. These are the traits and attributes you value the

THE HERO OF YOUR OWN LIFE

most in life.

- This is how you want to live your life.

_____

_____

_____

Your passion and purpose are in the answers above. You are the hero of your own life.

Creating the New You

You've unpacked your limiting thinking, figured out your why, and created new, empowering thinking as you climbed back up the transformational ladder. You have figured out your mission and what you're passionate about. Now it's time to take these new, empowering views, follow your bliss, and create the hero of your life. This part of the exercise will include creating powerful daily personal meditations and visualizations.

- Hold the image of you being or doing the things that you want this new you to be or do. You are the quantum creator, commanding matter to conftorm to your intentions.

- With clarity, hold the image of each manifestation in your mind for a few seconds, and then let it go into the quantum field to be executed by the Universe/God/Creator.

- Give up trying to figure out how or when or where or with whom. Know that your creation will come in a way that you will least expect. It will surprise you and leave no doubt that this came from a higher power.

When you are subconsciously skilled at something, it means you just do it without having to place a great deal of conscious thought or attention to the activity. This is what you want to have happen.

You want to practice being the new you so much that it becomes subconscious. The keys to meditation and visualization are to focus on frequency, intensity, and duration. The more you do it, the easier it gets. The better you can focus and concentrate, the easier it will be for you to tap into that particular mindset the next time. The longer you can linger in the thoughts and emotions of your new ideal without letting your mind wander to extraneous stimulus, the more you will memorize new thoughts and feelings.

Creating a New Reality

Your new personality should create a new reality. When you are being someone else, you naturally will have a different life. The new identity is no longer emotionally anchored to known situations in your life that keep recycling the same circumstances; therefore, it is a perfect place from which to envision a new destiny. This is the place you want to be to create your hero life.

The reason your past intensions hardly ever manifested is that you were trying to hold a mindful intention while being lost in lower emotions such as guilt, shame, sadness, unworthiness, anger, or fear connect to the old self. It was those feelings that were governing your thoughts and attitude. The 5 percent of your conscious mind was fighting against the 95 percent of your subconscious. Thinking one way and feeling another cannot produce results.

Creating a New Destiny

Now that you have released that old energy from the body, what do you want? Do you want to heal an area of your body or life? Do you want a loving relationship, a more satisfying career, a new car? Is your dream to write a book, to send your kids to college, or to go back to school yourself? From a new state of mind, body, and gratitude in a greater, more coherent energy, see these images in your mind of what you want to create in your new life. Craft the specific future events you want to experience by observing them into physical reality. You as the quantum observer are commanding matter to conform to your intentions. With clarity you will hold the image of each manifestation in your mind for a few seconds, and the let it go into the quantum field to be executed by your Universe/God/Creator.

Write down what you want now that you are the new you.

1. _____

2. _____

3. _____

4. _____

5. _____

It might be helpful to create six-month goals from this list. By putting dates on when you expect to have or be these new ideas you are giving the quantum field even more information to help it manifest with you. Of course, you still need to be surprised as to how or even when these events will occur. In fact, these areas might be manifested way before your goal date. Again, be as specific as you can be in what you want so you can visualize it and feel the joy and emotion of having achieved it in your life.

You are now ready to start your meditations. Now that you have worked through the transformational ladder, created a new you, and made your six-months goals, it's time to put it all together into one mediation that you can do every day.

Rehearsing the New You—System Overview

This is an overview of the entire medication/visualization method that, when practiced daily, will create the new you with new thoughts, emotions, and behaviors.

Part 1—The Induction Phase

It is time to relax the body and mind. The brain's electrical signals vary depending on what level of relaxation or arousal you are in. Alpha waves are generated when the brain is conscious but relaxed. Theta waves usually occur during sleep but can be induced when in deep meditation. Theta waves are the gateway to learning, memory, and intuition.

Progressive muscle relaxation is a great way to get the mind into alpha or theta waves which are extremely conducive to the power of suggestion. The best way to do this is to do a guided body relaxation meditation. This is essentially what hypnotherapists do.

Part 2—Remind Yourself Who You Don't Want to Be

Once your brain is in alpha or theta, pick one emotion (at a time) and associated thoughts, feelings, actions, and behaviors that you want to be rid of. Remind yourself of the emotions, feelings, and behaviors you use to think and feel and ask the Universe/God/Creator to take this emotion away from you. You can find these lists in your Transformational Ladder exercises.

Part 3—Create the New You

Take what you have answered in the Creating the New You exercises and feel into the new you. How you will think and act. Think about being like this new person. Picture yourself acting, doing, and saying what this new you would say and do.

Part 4—Visualize What the New You Wants

Picture the images in your mind and feel how you would feel with the new areas in your life. What's going on around you? What are people saying or doing with you? Feel the emotion of having and doing this new behavior.

Part 5—Release the Vision

Release your new vision of you to the Universe/God/Creator and ask for a sign that you made a connection.

Part 6—Give Thanks

Give thanks for having or being this new person. Be in so much gratitude and live in that gratitude all day long.

Part 7— Live as If

Live the rest of the day as if you are that new person and have such gratitude for the life you are living as this new person with this new behavior.

Hero Life

Hero Life is J. Scott MacMillan's coaching and education business. He specializes in helping people become their true, authentic, and mission-driven selves through coaching and education programs. His website is www.jscottmacmillan.com.

Acknowledgments

There are many people in my life that have been a part of who I have become that I would like to thank. First and foremost I'd like to thank my parents for always being there for me and always keeping the faith. I want my children to know they are and will always be great inspiration and joy in my life. Last but not least I want to thank all the great muses in my life. For some authors there is one person or one song or movie that provides creative inspiration to put pen to paper. For me it has been the amazing and beautiful women in my life. Every relationship provided sincere and deep love that changed me in fundamental ways. The words on these pages are primary responses to relationships that needed to move on but provided deep personal reflection and awareness that put me on a path to becoming a more mindful and authentic person.

Made in United States
North Haven, CT
19 April 2022

18362571R00131